The Undertaker's Nightmare!

Ray Comfort

The Undertaker's Nightmare!
ISBN 1-878859-11-0
Library of Congress Card #94-075509
Non-copyright June, 1994
Living Waters Publications
P.O. Box 1172
Bellflower
CA 90706

Cover art—Fred Gonzales

Cover design—Jesse Gonzales
Graphics II
402 South Park Blvd;
San Antonio
TX 78204

Printed in the United States

Dedication

This book is dedicated to my friends Jesse and Lydia Gonzales. My special thanks to my lovely wife Sue, for her help and patience, and to my friend Stephen Smith and his mom, Gloria, for their editorial assistance.

Also my sincere thanks to Harry Brut of Brut Printing in Jacksonville, Florida, for his generosity in making this publication possible.

FOREWORD

One Mightier Than I is Coming

"I indeed baptize you with water; but One mightier than I is coming, whose sandal strap I am not worthy to unloose. I am not the Christ, but I have been sent before Him. He who has the bride is the bridegroom; but the friend of the bridegroom, who stands and hears him, rejoices greatly because of the bridegroom's voice. Therefore this joy of mine in fulfilled. He must increase, but I must decrease. He who comes from above is above all; he who is of the earth is earthly and speaks of the earth. He who comes from Heaven is above all. And what He has seen and heard, that He testifies; and no one receives His testimony. He who has received His testimony has certified that God is true. For He whom God has sent speaks the words of God, for God does not give the Spirit by measure. The Father loves the Son, and has given all things into His hands. He who believes in the Son has everlasting life; and he who does not believe the Son shall not see life, but the wrath of God abides on him" (Luke 3:16, John 3:28-36).

John, Son of Zacharias—Forerunner to the Christ, AD 26, Wilderness of Judea.

"Most assuredly, I say to you, if anyone keeps My word he shall never see death."

Jesus of Nazareth

Contents

Based on the Gospel of John

Chapter One
The Town of Hatedog

A young preacher, fresh out of Bible college stood up in the pulpit to give his first sermon. As he neared the end of his message, he kept in mind the words of Billy Graham, as he informed his hearers as to what he was about to do. The famous preacher would say, "In a few moments I'm going to ask you to stand on your feet and bow your head." So, in a clear voice the young preacher said, "There is a conviction of the Spirit of God on this congregation. In a few moments, I'm going to ask you to stand on your heads and bow your feet."

I once wanted to speak of the sacrifice of the sinful woman in scripture who washed Jesus' feet with her tears, and dried them with the hair of her head, by soberly saying " . . . and this woman washed Jesus' hair with her feet!"

Sometimes our words don't exactly convey what we originally planned. Many times I have felt unspeakably inadequate to relate what is on my heart. I have wanted to impart the incredible truths of the Gospel of Salvation, and I'm sure, I have ended up making about as much sense to my hearers as our young preacher in his first pulpit.

The problem not only lies with the preacher, but also with the hearer. Without the help of God's Spirit to give us light and lead us into truth, the most "enlightened" of us sits in dim darkness. Even the opening words of the Gospel of John will be but dark and dead letters to us without the light and life of the Spirit. They tell us of our origin, yet without the help of God, they will more than likely be written off by a carnal mind as a mere man made mundane myth.

A true story was told of a young soldier in the civil war. After an explosion left him seriously injured, he lay on the battlefield, covered in blood.

A male nurse sat beside the helpless trooper, holding his thumb on the man's neck to stop the bleeding.

In the heat of battle, a doctor came

alongside the two men. He looked closely at the wound and told the soldier that he was very fortunate. The damage was very close to a main artery, and if that had been severed he would have died almost immediately.

The doctor carefully stitched the small veins over which the nurse had applied pressure.

A few minutes later, he was called back. The terrified nurse was holding his thumb over a main artery which had suddenly burst. The good doctor explained that he could now do nothing for the soldier. As soon as the nurse removed his thumb, blood would gush out rapidly and there was no way he could contain its flow.

Over the next three hours, the brave young soldier thanked the nurse for what he had done for him, wrote farewells to his loved ones, put his house in order, then told the nurse to remove his thumb. The horrified nurse turned his face away from the young warrior, removed his thumb, and the soldier was dead within three minutes.

Whether we are enlightened to understand it or not, the eternal God of Creation holds our life in His hands. When the preserving presence of His hand is removed, we die. We are but mortal human beings, and "in Him we live and move and have our being." Every breath we take, and every heart beat that follows, comes only because He keeps His gracious hand upon our lives.

He alone is the origin of human life, the One who sustains our very existence.

Yet, we live in a world which has rejected the biblical account of creation, and is therefore in darkness as to its origin. But to the unthinking mind, there is no dilemma. We just happen to be here. We are merely elevated animals which have, over millions of years, evolved from a puddle of nothingness. Like a shallow-thinking animal, life is nothing more than a mere "eat, drink and fetch the ball, for tomorrow we die."

For those who grope in the darkness for purpose of existence, life itself becomes a nightmare. If there is no *reason* for existence, then suffering and pain, life, love and laughter have no point. Loved ones will be torn from our hands by the grave, and there is nothing we can do about it but wait for our turn! We stand like a dumb dog on a walled and busy freeway in the town of Hatedog.

Look at these pitiful and hopeless words from the famed Bertrand Russell:

"The life of man is a long march through the night, surrounded by invisible foes, tortured by weariness and pain, towards a goal that few can hope to reach, and where none may tarry long. One by one as they march, our comrades vanish from our sight, seized by the silent orders of omnipotent death."

To the ungodly, death is Omnipotent, Almighty and Sovereign. It towers over them like a tormenting monster, casting its dark and evil shadow over their fruitless and fading futility.

He Calls the Tune

Rejection of the Bible's account of creation as given to us in the Book of Genesis, could rightly be called "Genecide," because it has eradicated the purpose of existence and left a whole generation with no certainty as to its beginning. Consequently, theory tales as to our origin have crept like primeval slime, from the minds of those who have an echo when they think. This intellectual genocide has given the godless a temporary license to labor to the extremes of its imagination, giving birth to painful conjecture as to human beginning. They speak in *speculation*, the uncertain language of those who drift aimlessly across the endless sea of secular philosophy.

The Scriptures, on the other hand, deal only with truth and certainty. They talk of fact, reality, and purpose for man's existence. The raging sea of futility retreats where the lighthouse of Genesis begins.

There was once a guest speaker at a large church, who listened as the congregation sang a well-known worship song slightly different from the way he had learned it. He had a sense of impatience as he thought to himself that the congregation had erred from the original tune. He determined to correct them before he preached. Fortunately for him, just before he conducted his foot into his musical mouth, the song leader said, "I love that chorus. And I thank God for allowing me to write it."

The world is full of people who, with a sense of impatience, would dare sing of what should and shouldn't be. However, God wrote the song and He calls the tune, whether we know it or not. His Word tells us, not only what should and shouldn't be, but what the future holds and what has been in the past. It is in the opening chapters of the Book of Genesis and the Gospel of John we see the true harmony of our origins.

John tells us that the Word, the "cause," was manifested when God said, "Let there be light." It was the *voice* of God which was the cause of all things. It was the Word which induced creation to be revealed from infinite nothingness.

Furthermore, we are told that the *life source* was revealed to humanity in human form; God, the Creator, was personified in Jesus of Nazareth. Modern science is thrown into rapture when it finds an ancient human skull from past ages. Delirious scientists make no bones about the fact that they think this is a step to uncovering the "mystery" of our origins; and from that, they try and piece together a flimsy skeleton of truth.

The bonafide truth, however, is no mystery. Human beings and all that surrounds them, were brought into being by the Voice of the Creator. Man wasn't the product of a big bang which came with no cause, no rhyme nor reason. The fuse of the big bang was sparked by the voice of God—Jesus Christ, the Word pre-incarnate. The Scriptures say of the Son:

"For by Him all things were created that are in Heaven and that are on the earth, visible and invisible, whether thrones or dominions or principalities or powers. All things were created through Him and for Him" (Colossians 1:16).

The "Word" spoken of by John produced life, because He had life in Himself. As we will see, this was His continual claim. Look at His unprecedented words: "I am the way the truth and the *life*," "I am come that they might have *life*," "I am the resurrection and the *life*." The Apostle Paul (who wrote most of the New Testament) said, "Christ, who is our *life*," while John wrote later, "He that has the Son has *life*."

In Him was life, and "the life was the light of men." This is why Jesus said strange things about His voice. He told his disciples not to marvel, because the hour was coming when *all* that were in their graves would hear His voice. He said, "My words are spirit, they are life," and all who accept Him, receive the *life* of God, and become "partakers of the inheritance of the saints in light" (Colossians 1:12).

Split Heirs

A true story is told of a millionaire who had a portrait of his beloved son painted before the son went to war. He was tragically killed in battle, and shortly afterward, the heart-broken millionaire died.

His will stated that all his riches were to be auctioned, specifying that the painting must sell first.

Many showed up to the auction, where a mass of the rich man's wealth was displayed. When the painting was held up for sale, there were few bids made. It was an unknown painting by an unknown painter of the rich man's uncelebrated son, so sadly, there was little interest.

After a few moments, a butler who worked for the man remembered how much the millionaire loved his son, decided to bid for it, and purchased the portrait for a very low price.

Suddenly, to everyone's surprise the auctioneer brought down his hammer and declared the action closed. The rich man's will had also secretly specified that the person who cared enough to purchase the painting of his beloved son was also to be given all the riches of his will.

This is precisely what God has done through the Gospel. He who accepts the beloved Son of God also receives all the riches of His will—the gift of eternal life and "pleasure forevermore." They become "joint heirs" with the Son.

As we will see further in this publication, this uncelebrated Son of God created havoc for undertakers by speaking to their frigid merchandise. His voice was supernatural. A mere "Lazarus come forth," that was spoken to a corpse (John 11:43), meant a nightmarish dilemma for the Bethany funeral director, because he was left with no body to deal with. Up until that moment, his business was mortally secure. Four days after the death, he had everything wrapped up, when suddenly, three words unraveled his inanimate toil. Reimbursement of all funeral expenses was just the beginning of the bad dream. Death was his living, and if this stranger from Nazareth continued to speak around graves, his business itself would soon be terminal. Jesus Christ was the undertaker's nightmare *because death bowed its vile knee to His voice, and the day is promised when all undertakers will hit the unemployment line!*

The raising of Lazarus snatched the profit from the undertaker, but the incident happened *for* the inestimatable profit of humanity. It was the long-awaited fulfillment of that which was spoken of by the prophets of old. It was a beam of wondrous and glistening light in the most hopeless and darkest of all caves.

I was once waiting to speak in a classy, traditional, but *live* church. Everything was so well run, from the opening prayer, to the notices, to the professional-sounding choir. All was efficiently managed that is, right up until the choir finished.

As the singers left the stage, the pulpit stood silently for what seemed an eternity. Someone had obviously slipped up on the order of service. Whatever or whoever was next hadn't come through. Typical. It doesn't matter how slick things run, it is always open to human error. It was unusual though, because every event was so flawlessly arranged up until that moment. Suddenly, one by one, heads began to turn and look directly at me. Strange. More people turned and stared, some with polite smiles and nods.

My eyes suddenly widened—*I was next on the agenda!* I grabbed my Bible and ran down the aisle, much to the amusement of the congregation.

There was also a long period of prophetic silence until John appeared and introduced the Messiah. John the Baptist gave the foreword to the pre-existent Jesus of Nazareth. He told his hearers that this was the One who was to come to earth with a pardon in His hand. He was the One who came to fulfill the Law of Moses, to satisfy its holy demands and redeem us from the curse of the Law by becoming a curse for us.

Intellectual Wimps

John had his own followers, but his light was merely a small and humble moon in contrast to the sun. His glow was not his own, but a pale reflection of the brilliant light of the Son of God; the perfect Lamb, without spot or blemish, who came from God to unlock the door of immortality.

When two of John's disciples heard him as he pointed to the Lamb, they followed Jesus. When they inquired about where He was staying, He just said, "Come and see," and so John's disciples left him to follow Jesus, and stayed with Him for the rest of the day. Andrew, one of them, found his brother Peter and brought him to Jesus. As soon as Peter met the Lord, Jesus looked at him, knew him, and told him that he was a stone.

The next day Jesus called Philip to follow Him, then Philip found Nathanael and told him about the Savior. Nathanael's *Can any good thing come out of Nazareth?*, is a typical reaction of the contemporary world to those who follow the Savior. To the cynical, Christians are intellectual wimps, prudes, rejects—

unlearned cripples who need some sort of crutch to get them through life. So it is understandable for them to ask, "Can any good thing come out of Christianity?" Down through the ages, its good name has been tainted with the stained brush of hypocrisy, dead religion, and more recently, fanatical sects and televangelism.

Philip merely answered Nathanael's cynicism with the same thing Jesus said to his brother—"Come and see." Skeptic, come and see. Atheist, come and see. Intellectual, come and see. Just come and see, and you who are blind will see. Come with a humble and teachable heart, and you who are sightless *will* understand and know, that this Man from Nazareth is the Son of God.

Hot Ham

My wife Sue was once shopping at the local supermarket, when a woman (who was obviously into word association) called to her from the cash register and said, "Excuse me, *Mrs. Cosy!*" The *Reader's Digest* mailed me a letter addressed to "Roy Compost." I trust it was a computer error and not word association.

When Nathanael however, decided to

see for himself and approached Jesus, the Lord showed that His knowledge of him was not mere human superficiality. He knew that he was a Jew who loved God and lived without guile and self-deceit. Here was a godly Jew, who would crawl over hot ham to find truth.

In Isaiah 11:1-3, the Scriptures tell us that the Messiah would have "quick understanding in the fear of the Lord; and He shall not judge after the sight of His eyes, neither reprove after the hearing of His ears." This was the case with Nathanael.

Jesus told him he would see the heavens open and angels ascending and descending upon the Son of God. Before him stood Jacob's true ladder. This was Israel's avenue to Heaven, the way, the truth, and the life.

Perhaps you are a little like Nathanael. Life's harsh realities have made you a little skeptical. You know that Jesus of Nazareth was unique, a good man, an exceptional teacher . . . *but is He God in human form?* Can a person really know, without doubt, they have eternal life? If you have misgivings, doubts, questions, then "come and see" as you read the following pages, and look closely at the most amazing Man to ever walk the paths of this dry, dark and dusty earth.

Chapter Two
The Sign of Fine Wine

Jesus probably wasn't much different than any other Jew at the wedding of Cana. This was the son of Mary, the 30 year old carpenter who had a group of friends who followed Him. The guests didn't know Him as a miracle-worker, because he hadn't yet performed any miracles. His mother however, knew who He was. She had many things, experiences, strange memories of Jesus, which she pondered in her heart. She remembered the appearance of the angel at the birth of Jesus, the wise men who brought gifts to Him when He was a child. She recalled His strange words spoken as a child, about being about His "Father's business."

Perhaps she spent many hours sitting at His feet, hearing gracious words pour from His lips. No doubt, when she had fears, problems and concerns, she gave them to Jesus, and listened to His incredible wisdom. So, it was not unusual for her to turn to Him at a time of need, and tell Him that the wedding's host had run out of wine.

What He said probably made no sense to her, but she knew not to question Him. His gentle rebuke, "Woman, what does your concern have to do with Me? My hour has not yet come," didn't make her withdraw in rejection, but provoked her to say to the servants, "Whatever He says to you, do it." Some say that she was wanting Jesus to reveal who He was through a miracle, and thus vindicate her of the reproach she had carried since His conception. Whatever the case, her words are as wise as can come from the lips of mortal humanity. Her bid holds the key to immortality. If Jesus says it, we should do it, because it can only be to our eternal welfare.

The wedding of Cana is a type of the Kingdom of God. In Matthew 22:3-22, Jesus likened the Kingdom to a wedding at which servants gathered the guests. Notice that Jesus and His "disciples" were invited. A Christian *is* a disciple. If someone is not disciplined to Jesus, if Jesus is not his "Lord," he will be cast out of *the* wedding into outer darkness. If we continue in His word, then are we His disciples indeed (John 8:31-32), and we are therefore invited to the Marriage Supper of the Lamb and will drink the fruit of the vine with Him in His Kingdom (Luke 22:18).

The ears of the servants were primed to the voice of the Son of God. When He told them to fill the pots with water, they filled them to the brim, and if we are servants of Christ we should do all we can for Him with whole-heartedness. If Jesus tells us to dig a hole, we should dig it deep. If He tells us to climb a mountain, we should climb it to the top, and if He tells us to fill waterpots with water, we should fill them to the brim.

When Jesus told them to draw the water out, they did so, and at His instruction, they took it to the master of the feast. The obedient don't yield to reason. Why should they take *water* to the master? But He said it, so they did it. They didn't question what He told them to do, and when they did what He said, they were witnesses to the first miracle of the Son of God on earth. These mere servants were eye witnesses of "His glory."

There is also a deeper explanation to this incident. This was the same God, who through Moses turned water into blood, who was turning water into wine. Here is a "typology" of the Old and the New Covenants:

1. The turning of water into blood was the first of the public miracles that Moses did in Egypt (Exodus 7:20), and the water into wine was the first of the public miracles that Jesus did in the world (John 1:11).

2. The signs that God gave to Egypt in the Old Testament were plagues, destruction and death, and the signs Jesus did in the world in the New Testament were healings, blessings and life.

3. The turning of water to blood initiated Moses (a type of the Savior—Deuteronomy 18:15) leading his people out of the bondage of Egypt into an earthly liberty, and the turning of water into wine initiated Jesus taking His people out of the bondage of the corruption of the world into the glorious liberty of the children of God (Romans 8:29).

4. The turning of water to blood culminated in the firstborn of Egypt being delivered *to* death, while turning the water into wine culminated in the life of the Firstborn being delivered *from* death (Colossians 1:18).

5. The Law was a ministration of death, the Gospel a ministration of life. One was written on cold tablets of stone, the other on the warm fleshly tablets of the heart. One was a ministration of sin unto condemnation and bondage, the other a ministration of righteousness unto life and liberty (2 Corinthians 3:7-9).

6. When Moses changed the water into blood, we are told that all the fish in the river died. When Jesus initiated the New Covenant, the catch of the fish are made alive in the net of the Kingdom of God (Matthew 4:19).

7. The river of blood was symbolic of death for Egypt, but the water into wine is symbolic of life for the world. The letter of the Law kills, but the Spirit makes alive (2 Corinthians 3:6).

8. When Moses turned the waters of Egypt into blood, the river reeked, and made the Egyptians search for another source of water supply (Exodus 7:21). When the Law of Moses does its work in the sinner, it makes life odious for him. The weight of sin on his back becomes unbearable as he begins to labor and be heavy-laden under its weight. Like the Egyptians, he begins to search for another spring of water; he begins to "thirst for

righteousness," because he knows that without a right standing with God, he will perish.

9. Moses turned water into blood, and Jesus' blood turned into water (1 John 5:6). They both poured from His side on the cross (John 19:34), perhaps signifying that both Law and Grace found harmony in the Savior's death—"Mercy and truth are met together; righteousness and peace have kissed each other" (Psalm 85-:10).

10. The water of the old covenant ran out. It could do nothing but leave the sinner with a thirst for righteousness. But as with the wine at Cana, God saved the best until last. The new wine given on the Day of Pentecost (Acts 2:13, Ephesians 5:18) was the Bridegroom giving us the "new" and "better" covenant (Hebrews 8:5-6).

The Bitter Cup

When we thirsted for life, as at Cana, Jesus freely furnished the sweetest of wines, but the terrible irony is that when He thirsted while in the bitterness of His suffering, He was given the most sour of wines (John 19:29). Yet, though the anguish of the cross would come by the hand of man, it was in truth a cup that the Father had given Him to drink, that we might be saved. This was the "hour" Jesus spoke of at the wedding, this was the purpose for which He was born.

Holy Muscle

When Jesus went to the temple, He found it to be filled with those buying and selling merchandise. According to the Jewish historian Josephus, at each passover, over 250,000 animals were sacrificed. The priests sold licenses to the dealers and therefore would have had a great source of income from the passover. When the Bible called them "changers of money," it was an appropriate term.

Jesus took a whip, overturned the money-changers tables and cleared the temple of those who had turned it into a "den of thieves." Its cleansing shows the strength of the character of Jesus of Nazareth. Here is a "man's man," flexing the muscle of holiness in a world of compromise.

There is, however, another theft going on in another temple. Mankind was made as a dwelling place for his Creator. God made him a little lower than the angels, crowned him with glory and honor, and set him over the works of His hands (Hebrews 2:7), yet sin has given the dwelling place to the devil. The thief, who came to kill, steal and destroy is making merchandise out of mankind. Instead of the heart of man being a temple of the Living God—a house of prayer—iniquity has made it a den of thieves.

When someone repents and calls upon the name of Jesus Christ, He turns the tables on the devil. The ten stinging cords of the Ten Commandments in the hand of the Savior, cleanses the temple of sin.

The alternative to cleansing the temple is judgment. If our temple is not purged of sin, it will end up in ruins. It was in the year 70 A.D. that the temple of Jerusalem was destroyed in judgment, and, if God is willing, we will only have 70 years on this earth. If we don't repent, Jesus warned that we will perish. No stone will be unturned on the Day of Wrath, except the "stone of stumbling," the stone which the builders rejected, *and all who shelter in Him.*

The Ten Commandments can also clear the compromising Church of God today. The problem with the buyers and the sellers in Jerusalem, was that they had lost sight of the fear of God. The temple was no longer a place of their holy Creator, but a mere means of gain, and so it is with many within the Church today. They have perverted the Gospel and preached that gain is godliness, from whom you and I are exhorted to "turn away" (1 Timothy 6:5).

But the crack of the whip of the Law has a way of bringing back the fear of God into the midst of the Temple. It has a way of reminding us of the God of Moses, of the thunderings and lightnings of Mount Sinai.

A new respect for the Law of God has always preceded revival in the Church. When the House of God is filled with covetousness, adultery, theft, lying, hatred, backbiting and strife, the snap of the scourging whip puts the terror of the Lord back into the House of the Lord, making it the House of Prayer that it should be.

Charles Spurgeon had a resolute grasp of the Law. In preaching to sinners, he said,

> "I would that this whip would fall upon your backs, that you might be flogged out of your self-righteousness and made to fly to Jesus Christ and find shelter there."

When the fire of zeal for God's House

flashed in the eyes of Jesus, He cried, "Take these things away! Do not make My Father's House a house of merchandise!", to which the Jews demanded a sign from Him that God was His Father.

How could this man speak on behalf of Almighty God they thought they knew so well!

They said they served the God of Israel, but in truth they served mammon.

Change of Heart

Jesus said that no man can serve two masters. We will either love God or we will love money; the one we beckon to is the one we bow to. This was clearly illustrated recently when I went down to the local courts to share my faith, a place I regularly go to chat with people. One man who was paying off court fines by working in the parking lot, proved to be very anti-Christian, so I was polite to him but gave him a wide berth each time I saw him.

I spoke to a couple of people and noticed that Mr. Nasty was also talking to his friends, no doubt warning them about me. As usual, I went to slip tracts under the windshield wipers of cars as I was leaving.

I had done this with hundreds of cars, with never one complaint from a soul.

As I lifted the wiper on the first vehicle, I heard one of Mr. Nasty's friends holler, "Don't put one of those #!@!!** things on my @!**$! truck." I immediately lifted the wiper and took back the tract and smiled at the guy. Then I got my wallet out, and as I did so I heard, "*I said don't !#$!!* put any of that !$!!+*! stuff on my @!$$*!* truck!*" I ignored him, got some money out of the wallet and slipped it under his windshield wiper. The tone of his voice altered completely, and he called a friendly, "*Hey thanks!*"

It was the change from my wallet that produced the change in his heart, and revealed the god to whom he immediately bowed.

When God speaks, the godly yield to His Lordship and conform to His word, and when the god of money speaks, the ungodly compromise their convictions and fall prostrate in allegiance.

That incident even changed Mr. Nasty's attitude towards me. The next time I saw him, he said of his friend, "*He couldn't believe you did that!*" From then on, he even waved to me when I arrived at the courts each day.

The Coming Hour

Jesus then said some strange words about the fact that He was going to raise His own body from the dead. The cross was ever before Him because He knew that He had come to suffer. This is why He previously said to Mary, "My hour is not yet come." He had a baptism to be baptized with, and He could never be truly at ease until man's greatest enemy, death, had become His footstool. Jesus referred to His "hour" seven times in the Gospel of John.

The Jews had no idea what Jesus was speaking about. Scripture enlightens us to the fact that when He told them He would raise the "temple" three days after they had destroyed it, He was actually speaking of His own body.

The religious leaders were like a man born blind, trying to understand color and light.

His disciples had light though. Jesus opened their understanding, and when they were born of the Spirit, the door cracked open wide to let the full sunlight of revelation fill their minds. They remembered that Jesus said He would raise the temple in three days, and they believed the Scriptures and the words which Jesus had said.

From that time on, He began doing miracles, which caused many to put their trust in Him for their eternal well-being. But Jesus didn't count the decision cards, because salvation is more than an intellectual ascent; true believers *continue* in His word. Jesus of Nazareth kept Himself back from them. He only draws near to those who draw near to Him. He knew what was in the heart of man—that one day they may cry "Hosanna!" and the next day, "Crucify Him!"

Chapter Three
Pounding the Mouth

It was Charles Finney who said that the Law was "the only just rule by which the guilt of sin can be measured." Nicodemus was one of many Jews to inch himself up against the straight-edge and perceive himself to be crooked. He realized his guilt, and was ushered to Christ by the "schoolmaster" of God's Law. He was humbled and brought to nothing by the Law, as was Nathanael, and the Jews on the Day of Pentecost.

A well-known magazine once ran an article which illustrated the difference between what a doctor says, and what he actually means. For example, if he said, "I'd like to run this test again," he really meant, "The lab lost your blood sample."

When he says, "Insurance should cover most of this," he is saying, "You will have to sell your house to cover the rest," and his, "Why don't you go over your symptoms with me one more time," actually is, "I can't remember who you are."

Jesus *knew* Nicodemus, unlike most of us who have trouble even remembering what day it is, let alone someone's name. He knew him, and He even knew what he had come to Him for. On the surface, when he approached the Savior, he didn't seem to be asking a question, and yet Jesus answers it as such. How can a partially blind man see his way clear? He stumbles in the semi-dark, and yet he is longing for clear light. Nicodemus had been given light enough by the Law to bring him to the feet of the Savior.

All Nicodemus said was that He thought Jesus came from God. This was a simple but profound statement from this godly Jew. He was acknowledging that Jesus was pre-existent, that He was the Holy One of Israel, that He was the promised Messiah. Jewish tradition taught him that he had already attained salvation merely by being born a Jew, yet his own heart told him he was a sinner, so Jesus spoke straight to his need. He saw Nicodemus lying beaten by the Law, shut up by its strict demands, and so He carefully took this bruised reed in His gentle hands (Matthew 12:20).

Like Paul, the Law had pounded Nicodemus until his bloodied mouth of justification could speak no more. Each holy Commandment beat him to a pulp and left him bruised, lying helplessly on the road to Jericho. He was exposed and undone, and the words of Jesus were oil and wine to his wounds.

The Law left Nicodemus hungering and thirsting for righteousness, longing to enter the Kingdom of God, so Jesus told him that to see God's Kingdom he had to be born again.

The more he strove to keep the Law, the more he saw that he fell short of its perfect requirements. The closer he went to the mirror, the more he saw his moral imperfections. His conscience knew that the desires of his sinful heart were abhorrent to God. He fell infinitely short of the Law's demand that he love his neighbor as much as he loved himself. As he looked into the perfect Law of liberty, it showed him that sin was exceedingly sinful. He needed a righteousness that exceeded the righteousness of the scribes and Pharisees to enter the Kingdom of God.

When a teacher of Israel heard these

strange words from *the* Teacher of Israel, he asked what they meant—how could a man enter his mother's womb a second time and be "born again?" This natural man was in the natural domain, so Jesus opened the door of the spiritual realm. He told him of the necessity of the new birth, that flesh is flesh, human is human, and Divine is Divine, that flesh and blood could not inherit the Kingdom of God (1 Corinthians 15:50). They were different kingdoms. Nicodemus must have a Divine operation to cut away his sinful heart before he could enter the Kingdom of God.

Suddenly, Jesus said curious things again. He began to talk in plurality saying, "We speak what we know and testify what we have seen, and you do not receive Our witness." This was the same Plurality who said, "Let Us make man in Our image, according to Our likeness" (Genesis 1:26). This was the "three who bear witness in Heaven: the Father, the Word, and the Holy Spirit; and these three are one" (1 John 5:7).

Nicodemus was bound by his natural, unbelieving and sinful heart. He needed Divine surgery. His circumcision must be "of the heart, in the Spirit and not of the letter" (Romans 2:29).

He told Nicodemus of His pre-existence, that He "came down from Heaven," He then spoke of the cross once again. For this purpose the Son of God was manifest, that He might destroy the works of the devil. He became flesh to pass through death, that through death He might "destroy him who had the power of death, that is the devil," and deliver those who through the fear of death, were all their lifetime slaves to its terror. He was "made a little lower than the angels, for the suffering of death," and as Moses held the serpent up in the wilderness for Israel to be healed, so Jesus of Nazareth must become a curse, to redeem us from the curse of the Law. The Law, like a vicious serpent, has a deathly bite for all who transgress its holy requisites.

It was Moses who held the serpent up on a pole, and it was Moses who put the Messiah on the cross. Jesus didn't come to obliterate the Law and the prophets— He didn't come to destroy, but to fulfil (Matthew 5:17). It was our transgressions that necessitated the Savior. If we hadn't sinned, there would have been no need for the cross. We broke the Law, and Jesus paid the fine. God loved the world with such passion, He sent His only Son to the cross of Calvary, so that we might trust in Him and Him alone, and in doing so, not perish under the wrath of His Law, but have everlasting life.

The cross was an evident token of the love of the Creator for His creation. He was in Christ, reconciling the world to Himself.

God didn't send His Son into the world to condemn the world. The Law had already done that. The Commandments thundered through the earth to show the criminal that he stood guilty before the Judge. Now He leaves His bench, comes down to the lowly criminal and pays the fine for him. If the criminal refuses the pardon, then he is still condemned by the Law.

In one sense, Jesus and the Law can't be separated. The Law is the express image of His holy nature. Both the Law and our God are "perfect, holy, just and good" (Romans 7:12, Psalm 19:7), and both are light (Proverbs 6:23, John 8:12). John Wesley, in speaking of the Christian's attitude to the Law, said,

> "Yea, love and value it for the sake of Him from whom it came, and of Him to whom it leads. Let it be thy glory and joy, next to the cross of Christ. Declare its praise, and make it honorable before all men."

All of humanity were condemned when God sent the light of His Law to stop our mouths, and leave the whole world guilty before Him (Romans 3:19). Jesus then said that we loved the darkness of sin rather than the light of righteousness, because the human heart found pleasure in sin. If you don't believe it, go and visit the "adult" section of your local video store. Look at the covers of the type of entertainment the heart of men and women crave for—unspeakable violence, inconceivable horror and unending sexual perversion. Yet, the violence and filth that pervades on video have the restraint of civil law on them. The influence of our laws holds back the depth of depravity to which man would sink. The mind boggles at what would happen if the bridle of civil law was taken from the straining neck of humanity. Even under its harness, America still manages a burglary every 11 seconds, a car theft every 20 seconds, a robbery every 47 seconds (in 1991, guns were used in 740,000 crimes) and a murder every 22 minutes—*that's 65 murders each day!* What would ensue if America's 544,000 (plus) police officers were suddenly removed from their duty, and humanity were told that if they followed their lawless hearts in any direction, into murder, rape, etc., there would be no consequence whatsoever? It would be then, that we would see how much men love darkness rather than light.

Unregenerate man feels about as comfortable in the light as a cat feels at a dog show. He far prefers to dance naked before the golden calf, than obey the precepts of the moral Law. It is only when the Ten Commandments are cast at the feet of this sinful world, and it hears words of wrath from a fiery-eyed Moses, that it will stop its festive and delirious dance with the devil.

The Cough Button

Most radio stations have something called a "cough button." This is a mechanism which may be pressed when the news reader or announcer desires to clear his throat. Without the listener being aware of it, the device kills the broadcast long enough for an unwanted frog to jump out of the news reader's throat.

In the mid-eighties, I had a friend who was an announcer with a local Christian radio station. His voice was deep, rich and refined. It had the distinguished sound of a high class British dignitary. My friend, at the time, had a problem with nasal congestion which I thought gave his voice an even deeper quality, with a richer sound to it.

One Sunday afternoon, I was in-studio as a guest on his show. With his usual eloquence, in his dignified way he introduced the program. I marveled at his sheer professionalism and his mastery over the English language. He then turned to me and said, "Today we have Ray Comfort in-studio . . . " and without any warning, leaned forward, pushed the "cough button," gave a most disgusting, loud and long "pig" sounding snort, then carried on without batting an eye, "Ray . . . welcome to the program." I was totally unprepared for that. I had never seen anything so funny in all my life. I couldn't answer him as I was bent over double, choking, and trying to catch my breath. Sue was listening to the program at home, mystified to the fact that all she could hear was a grunting, gagging sound in the background.

Most of the world has its own "kill switch." Until we are converted, we have disgusting things in our lives that we don't want the world to know about. Like the prodigal son who left his father and found himself in a pig sty, our heart's desire is for pig food. The trouble is, we are unaware that God is our "in-studio" guest, and He doesn't think our wicked heart is at all funny.

As an unregenerate young man, I remember staring at a famous plaque which said that Jesus Christ was "the silent listener to every conversation." It made me feel uncomfortable in my sinful state. I loved the darkness, and even a glimmer of light was disturbing to my soul.

Drawing the Curtains

After the discourse with Nicodemus, we are told that Jesus went to Judea and began to baptize there. John was also baptizing in Aenon near Salim, "because there was much water there." For years there has been much ado about how much water, and how believers should be baptized, but this is evidence for total immersion. If all that was required was a light sprinkling, then John need only have had a bowl of water to do thousands.

After a dispute between John's disciples and the Jews about purification, some came to John and told him that Jesus was getting more converts. Here was the test of John's heart. Was he a King Saul, who burned with jealousy that David had slain more than him, or did he have a humble heart? Did he mean his previous words about not being worthy to unloose the shoe straps of Jesus? His answer was revealing.

He said that a man cannot receive a thing unless God gives it to him, therefore what man can boast of anything? If you are not a Christian, and you think you are open-minded in reading this book, it is only because the One who created you has given you the grace to read it. The scientist who discovers the secrets of nature merely does so because of the ability given to him by God. The athlete who runs faster, jumps higher or further than others, only does so because of his God-given will and the ability to do so. The man who, through strength of character, climbs back up and makes his obstacles his stepping stones, only does so because God gave him such strength of character. Who of us can boast of anything? John knew this and immediately slammed the door on the arrogant face of pride.

The friend of the bridegroom who takes preeminence over the bridegroom is no true friend. If he cares for him, he will make sure he has his day of honor. John said that his ministry must decrease so that Jesus would increase. He was merely "the voice of one crying in the wilderness, preparing the way of the Lord" (Matthew 3:3), and the Greek word used for *voice* is "phone." The bridegroom's job was to be busy carrying messages from Heaven to earth, and his tone was one of true humility.

John knew that this was He who came from above, and he knew that he himself was merely from below. One was the Bridegroom from Heaven, the other, the voice of a friend from earth.

When the Bridegroom arrived, the voice was no longer needed on the line to prepare the way. He wasn't seeking an extension of his ministry, neither was he seeking to be put on "hold"—it was time for the phone to be disconnected.

Then John climaxes his ministry before the curtains were drawn. He said that all who receive Jesus, honor the Father. He also said that Jesus spoke the words of God, and that the Creator of the universe gave Jesus the Spirit without measure. The Father loved the Son, and He gave all things into His hands. All who trusted Jesus with their eternal salvation would never be disappointed. God's promise in Christ was everlasting life.

I was once sharing my faith with a young lady in her late teens, who thought a person would get to Heaven by being good. She also said that she didn't understand why Jesus died on the cross. Then she looked at me with wide eyes and said, "Some people once came down our street and *saved* me." When I asked if *she* thought she was saved, she said, "I hope so!"

Salvation comes through repentance, faith and from a surrender of the human will to the will of God, not through the persuasion of someone else's will to say a prayer. When John 3:36 says, "He that believes on the Son has everlasting life," the Greek word used for "believes" is "pistcuo," which means *to trust*. However, later in the verse it also contains the words "he that believes not shall not see life, but the wrath of God abides on him." This time the word used for "believe" is "apeitheo," which means "disobedient." The disobedient will not see the salvation of God, no matter what prayer they have prayed, because they refuse to surrender their will to the Lordship of Jesus Christ, who is "coming in flaming fire to take vengeance on those who know not God and *obey not the Gospel of our Lord Jesus Christ*" (2 Thessalonians 1:8, italics added). The word used in this case for "believe" means "to hear (as a subordinate)."

Chapter Four
Well Spoken

Most of us equate happiness with riches. It's the reason millions spend billions gambling in places like Lost Wages, Nevada. After all, who is happier—the man who has a full stomach, warm clothes, a nice safe house, and bills paid, or someone in the opposite state (Ohio)? Consequently, many will do almost anything for money.

Take the 32 year old man in Portland, Oregon, who was arrested by police after swallowing a $2,299 ring in an attempt to steal it from a supermarket variety store.

The ring showed up some time later when the man was taken to the hospital after complaining of intense abdominal pains. He obviously had a taste for fine jewelry.

Sometimes, money drops in our lap, such as the case of a woman named Zelma Neal from Rantoul, Illinois, who said she "squealed" with delight when she opened a new "shrink-wrapped" Bible and found six $100 bills between its pages. She said that she had left her Bible at home and so she pulled a new one from the church library and removed the plastic seal.

Most however, find that money doesn't come so easily, but in John chapter 4, we find a woman found that something fell into her lap that was infinitely more valuable.

It would seem that it was the knowledge that the Pharisees had heard that Jesus led John in the baptism tally, that caused Jesus to leave Judea for Galilee. Scripture tells us that He also had another motive—for some reason, He wanted to pass through Samaria.

He stopped at Jacob's well in the city of Sychar, near the piece of ground that Jacob gave to his son Joseph, and around the sixth hour, He rested His weary body by the well.

In time, a woman of Samaria came to the well to draw water, and heard Jesus say, "Give Me a drink." We are told that He had nothing with which He could draw water from the deep well, neither did He have His disciples with Him to give Him a drink, because they were away buying food. It was as though Jesus sent them all to buy food, because He wanted to speak alone with this woman. Sometimes it is beneficial to have a person alone when we speak to them of the things of God. Pride will often stop people from being open-hearted.

Jesus could have miraculously created a cup of fresh water in His hand, but He didn't because He wanted to use water to draw this woman to Himself.

She was taken back by His request, astounded that a Jew would even speak with what most Jews considered to be a low class "Samaritan."

We have, in the following dialogue, the right way to share the Christian faith.

1. The Master of evangelism began with that which was in the tangible realm—something she could relate to—water.

2. He then swung to the spiritual, the imperceptible, by saying that if she knew the gift of God, she would ask Him and He would give her living water. This woman, as a daughter of Adam, had a God-given thirst for immortality, but

she had no thirst for righteousness, made plainly evident by her sinful lifestyle.

When Jesus spoke of the truths of the Kingdom of God, like Nicodemus, she remained in the earthly realm. She thought He spoke of water from the well. It would take the grace of God to open her eyes and ears so that she could understand what Jesus was saying. No one can come to the Son, unless the Father draws him.

Jesus told her that those who drank from Jacob's well would thirst again. Jacob's well is like the world, and worldly pleasures are shallow, and can only quench for a moment. They promise but don't deliver. The world's water runs through the hands of humanity, and falls into the dry desert of futility, but whoever drinks of the water that Jesus Christ gives shall never thirst. The water that comes from the hands of the Son of God becomes a fountain of water, springing up into everlasting life.

The world's water is laden with salt. God's water is pure, fresh, clean, cool and refreshing, flowing from the throne of immortality.

3. The woman wanted the water, but it came only in the cup of holiness—the living waters run beside the paths of right-

eousness. She wanted to be free from death and futility, but she couldn't have eternal salvation until her iniquity was dealt with. She was in debt to the Law; she was found "wanting" in the balance. She must first be justified in Christ.

We are told that she was an adulteress. She hadn't only transgressed the Seventh Commandment *in spirit*, but she had committed adultery multiple times and the man she was now living with wasn't her husband. Jesus used this fact to bring the knowledge of sin, and she respected Him for His love and gentle forthrightness by perceiving that His words came from God.

The Law makes the sinner thirst after righteousness, and then the Gospel quenches the yearning in Christ.

Those who follow in His footsteps, and take the time to show sinners that they have sinned against God by transgressing His moral Law, will find that the sinner's conscience will almost always openly acknowledge the truth of the Commandment. This will often be reflected in a respect for the true and faithful witness of the Christian, if his testimony has been given in the gentleness and meekness of Christ.

Suddenly, this harlot opened her heart

and revealed a knowledge of spiritual things. She spoke of her forefathers who worshipped on Sychar's mountain, but the Jews worshipped in Jerusalem. Jesus answered her by speaking of an intimate relationship that each believer will have with the Father, after His redemptive work on earth is finished. Then, all who trust in Him will worship the Father in spirit and in truth.

A pastor who understood the importance of a sinner having a knowledge of sin, was once approached by his six year old son. The child said that he wanted to "ask Jesus into his heart." The father, suspecting that the child lacked the knowledge of sin told him that he could do so when he was older, then sent him off to bed.

A short time later, he got out of bed and asked his father if he could give his life to the Savior. The father still wasn't persuaded of the son's understanding, and not wanting the child's salvation to be spurious, he sent him back to his room.

A third time the son returned. This time the father questioned him as to whether he had broken any of the Ten Commandments. The young boy didn't think he had. When he asked him if he had lied, the child said he hadn't. The father thought for a moment, then asked him how many lies he had to tell to be a liar, and when it was established that one lie made the person a liar, the child thought for a moment, realized he had lied, then broke down in uncontrollable tears. When the father then asked him if he now wanted to "ask Jesus into his heart," the child cringed, and shook his head. He was fearful because he now had a knowledge that he had sinned against God. He could now do more than experimentally "ask Jesus into his heart," he could now find a place of godly sorrow, repentance towards God, and faith toward our Lord Jesus Christ.

Then the woman began to speak of the coming Messiah. The Law had obviously done its work. It had been a schoolmaster to bring her the knowledge of sin. It is only when sinners have been humbled by the Law, and have a knowledge of sin that they are ready for the Gospel of Salvation.

Shrimp Rolls

At this point of time, the disciples returned from the store and saw Him talking with the woman. They were amazed that He spoke to her because, not only was she a Samaritan, but she was a loose woman.

It was tradition that women were not to be addressed in public, nor were they even to be instructed out of the Law. However, the disciples had the good sense to hold their peace.

Just as Andrew found Peter, and Philip found Nathanael, so this woman could not contain the fact that she had met the Savior. The Bible tells that she left her waterpot. She had come to draw water, but now that didn't matter. Nothing of this world is worth pursuing in comparison to what we find in Jesus of Nazareth. The temporal fades as a leaf when compared to the eternal. All that pertains to this life is but grass; the grass withers, the flower fades, but the Word of God endures forever.

She had found the Word of God, the very Door to eternity, and her heart beat with excitement. No longer was it a declining heartbeat of hopelessness, waiting for death to seize upon it, but it was a new beat that God Himself had started, the heartbeat of immortality. She had come to draw water, and now her cup ran over. *She could not contain it*. As a new believer, she didn't join an evangelistic training school, nor did she wait until she had the right words. Instead, she went back to the men, more than likely some she had sinned with, and said, "Come and see a man who told me all things that I ever did. Could this be the Christ?" She had found the Light of the world, and she pointed others towards Him.

Meanwhile, His disciples were in another world, concerned with earthly things, so they urged Him to eat, but He had "food" they knew nothing of. Jesus was committed to reaching out to the lost, and said that to reach out to the unsaved was to do the will of the Father.

The fields are white for harvesting, but most of the Church is asleep in the barn. Satan has hidden the will of the Father from the majority of believers, because most don't see evangelism as being anywhere near the priority of the Church, yet it is number one.

If preachers put half as much emphasis on sowing and reaping in evangelism, as they do on money matters, we would certainly see a revival in the Church that would flow out into the world. Then perhaps we wouldn't even have to mention money matters. That's why Jesus said, "lift up your eyes." The Church doesn't see beyond itself, because its emphasis is wrong. May God set the barn in which it sleeps on fire. May the fires of an awaiting Hell stir the sleeping laborers to arouse and rush into the field of the world. We should be sowing and reaping, and gathering "fruit for everlasting life;" reaping where others have sowed, and sowing that others might reap. Jesus said, "I have sent you to reap that for which you have not labored," and all Christians have been "sent" with the words, "Go into all the world and preach the Gospel to every creature."

We once sent a Christian brother some evangelical tracts in a box we had obtained from our church food ministry. They often supplied us with boxes, and had given us some with a label on the side which read "shrimp spring rolls—keep refrigerated." Unfortunately, the man wasn't home when his tracts arrived. His sister saw "the label" and immediately put the box of tracts into the freezer.

It is the devil's agenda to put all evangelical literature and endeavors on ice. If you don't believe me, try and start an evangelical outreach in your church and see how warm the response is. It is an uphill battle because all Hell lets loose when the Church does what it is told to do.

I think there are two major reasons the Church doesn't reach out to the lost. Both are to do with fear. First, there is a lack of the fear of God. If we feared God, we would obey Him. But more than that, if we feared God, we would be terrified for those who are under His wrath. The Apostle Paul so rightly put his inspired finger on it when he said, "Wherefore knowing the terror of the Lord, we persuade men." Those who understand God's fitting fury against sin, will compel sinners to come into the Kingdom of God.

The second fear is the "fear of man." Most of us are more concerned about our own skin rather than our neighbors. Our acceptance with him is more important to us than his acceptance with God. The momentary heat of embarrassment to us is more consequential than his eternity in the lake of fire.

Jesus said, "Fear not: from henceforth you shall catch men" (Luke 10:5). It's appropriate that the "fear not" is there. How can we fear when we aren't the ones who should be fearful? What doctor would withhold a cure to cancer from his patient because of fear?

The woman of Samaria wasn't fearful of rejection. The Bible tells us that many

of the Samaritans believed in Jesus pure-
ly because of the testimony of the
woman. She didn't come to them with
eloquent words of men's wisdom; she
came with the true and faithful witness
of "He told me all that I ever did." The
men of the city knew all that she "did,"
and no doubt some remembered who she
did it with.

May God give each of us the courage
and the good sense to speak of the omni-
science of God. He sees all things we
do—"Shall not He who formed the eye
also see?" All things lie open and exposed
before the eyes of Him of whom we have
to give an account. God will bring every
work to judgment, including every secret
thing, whether it is good or evil. When
men and women understand that a holy
and wrath-filled God sees their every
thought and deed, coupled with the fact
that they have transgressed His Law, they
too will come to the Savior.

These new believers urged Jesus to
stay longer with them, so He gave them
two more days of His precious time, and
many more came to a knowledge of the
truth. Their faith in Him came, not only
because they believed the woman's
testimony, but they themselves had an
encounter with the Son of God, the
Christ, the Savior of the world.

Jesus then departed from Sychar and went to Galilee, where He was welcomed. It was then He said that a prophet has no honor in his own country, an obvious reference to the rejection of His ministry in Nazareth, where they tried to take His life (Luke 4:29).

The Nobleman's Nobility

A short time later, Jesus returned to Cana of Galilee, a place where He had gained a reputation after turning the water into wine. It was there that Jesus was besieged by a certain nobleman, a royal official whose son was lying ill at Capernaum, at the point of death. If the miracle-worker could change water into wine, surely He could heal his son.

When Jesus spoke to the father rebuking him for his unbelief, he was not deterred. Some may have tried to justify themselves, or be offended by such a reprimand, but not this man. His obvious love for his child was much more of a priority than his own welfare. His "mustard seed" of faith wasn't the greatest, but his love was strong, and Jesus therefore said to him, "Go your way, your son lives."

It was then that the nobleman nobly exercised faith in the words spoken by

Jesus. This was a personal word from the Lord, and when Jesus said something, it would be done.

On his way back home, he was approached by a servant who told him that his son was healed the very same moment at which Jesus said, "Your son lives"—no doubt, much to the nobleman's unspeakable delight.

Chapter Five
The Compulsive Lier

Jesus had been sent to the lost sheep of the House of Israel. While the Jews celebrated one of their many feasts in Jerusalem, the Good Shepherd made His way to one of His lost sheep who lay by the Sheep Gate at a pool called Bethesda. The pool had five porches in which a great multitude lay sick.

Here lay an array of the works of the devil. He came to kill, steal and destroy, and in these five porches was a five-fingered-display, a handful of his work. This great multitude spent their lives waiting in hope—for an angel to stir up the water, and first in was first served. Whoever stepped into the water as number one was healed of his disease, no matter what it was.

But a certain man lay in the shade of

the porch. He had been in infirmity for 38 years. When Jesus knew that he had been there for such a long time, He asked him what seems to be a ridiculous question. *Did he want to be healed?* When asked the question, the man gave reason for his not being healed: he was alone in life, and not a soul stood by him. He waited for the water to stir, but when he stirred himself and dragged his paralysed body towards the water, someone else would step in the pool in front of him, and be healed.

Life is like that for most. We are in the human race, and in this life, it is first in who is first served. The weak, the infirm, the lame, the blind and the poor are left behind, but this is not so in the Kingdom of God. Jesus is still in the table-turning business. He came to destroy the works of the devil, and He looked at this fallen son of Adam and said, "Rise, take up your bed and walk."

Immediately, the man was made well. The Word brought life as at the beginning. One word from Jesus and dead muscle came to life—bones became strong and healthy. He stood to his feet, picked up his bed and walked! For 38 years the man lay bound by disease; for 38 years life had passed him by, and with one word he was completely changed.

What a day of rejoicing that God had visited His people! Who could not rejoice? The Pharisees, that's who!

Jesus healed him on the Sabbath, and at His instruction, he picked up and carry his bed on the day of rest, something the Jews considered to be unlawful. So they interrogated the healed man, and found that he didn't even know who Jesus was. All he knew was that he had been told to pick the bed up, and he had done so and was healed. He was no longer a lier.

Later, Jesus found him in the temple. The man knew that it was God who healed him through this Stranger, therefore he made his way to the temple to give God thanks.

Those who have been saved by the Lord, know where to go. We once lay as feeble, fragile and frail folk, helpless and hopeless, pathetically paralyzed by the devil, "taken captive to do his will" until Jesus spoke a word to us. We were on a death-bed of sin with no one able to help us, but we heard the voice of the Word of God: "Arise from the dead, and Christ shall give you light."

Now a thankful heart for the unspeakable gift makes us want to be always in the presence of God. Unlike the healed man however, we need not go to the temple to thank the Father, for He has made His abode in the heart of the believer. The work of the cross has made the believer the temple of the Living God.

Perhaps, Jesus found him on his knees in the temple. It was there that He steered the man onto the path of righteousness. This man now had legs that could take him where his sinful heart had desired to take him for 38 years.

He was released from the prison of paralysis, and freed from the steel bars that stopped him lifting his hand to drink the sins the world so freely offers. It was there that Jesus gave Him one of the greatest gifts a Christian can have—the very well-spring of wisdom, the "fear of the Lord."

If this man's healthy feet caused him to sin, it would be better for him to be lame, than go to Hell in health. He said, "Go your way and sin no more, lest a worse thing come upon you."

Hard though it may be for us to conceive, there is something worse than spending our time on earth in the prison of disease and pain, and that is spending eternity in the torments of Hell where there is neither a friend to help you into the pool of Bethesda, nor the healing voice of the Son of God. All hope will be gone forever.

After the healing, the Jews stopped their feasting. They had something more important on their minds—murder!

Max Wax

As I thoroughly waxed my surfboard, a young and naive boy said, "You're putting on too much." "No I'm not," I thought. I knew what I was doing. There's nothing worse than slipping off a surfboard because of too little wax. Suddenly, I heard country and western music playing, and realized that I was only dreaming. I hadn't been surfing for years, and I had been woken before I had even wet my feet!

I was in a hotel in Dallas, Texas, and my inconsiderate neighbor had ruined my thoroughly enjoyable dream.

I glanced at the clock—*5:40 a.m.!* I was on Pacific Time. That meant it was actually 3:40 a.m. *Some "neighbor" this was.* The music sounded like it was right by my ear. Then I realized *it was right by my ear.* It was "my" radio alarm clock. This had happened before in another hotel. Obviously, the person in the room before me had set the alarm to catch an early plane, and had failed to turn it off.

That was how the "alarm" of the conscience of the Pharisee worked. It was his conscience, but it had been "set" by his religious peers. Rather than being established by the Law of God, its standard of morality was determined by the tradition of the elders, so that they could now plot murder in the name of their God, without the alarm of conscience.

The fact that Jesus had (in the Pharisee's mind) violated the Sabbath, sparked a fire of hatred within their hearts. He answered their accusations with, "My Father has been working until now, and I have been working."

The fire suddenly became a raging inferno, fueled by the fact that Jesus called God His Father, making Himself equal to God. If God was His Father, then He was His Son.

Jesus then began to speak the most profound words ever uttered by any human being. *Look at His claims.* Either this was God in human form, or a crackpot. There is no middle ground. He said:

1. Whatever He saw the Father do, He did.

2. God showed Jesus everything He did, and He had even more things to show Him, that would cause them to be astonished.

3. Just as God raised the dead and gave life to them, so Jesus gave life to whoever He would.

4. God Himself had appointed Jesus of Nazareth as the Judge of all mankind.

5. Humanity should honor Jesus, as much as they honor God.

6. Those who didn't honor Jesus, didn't honor God.

7. All who heard His words and trusted in the Father escape the wrath of the Law.

8. All who trusted Him passed from death into life.

9. The hour would come when everyone in their graves would hear the voice of Jesus, and be raised from the dead.

10. As God is the source of all life, so He has given Jesus life in Himself

He then zeroed in on the fact of Judgment Day. He warned that the Day would come when the same Word of God which brought creation into being, would bring life to those in their graves, so that Eternal Justice might be manifest. The grave will not hide men from the Justice of Almighty God. All humanity will have their day in court, and on that Day there will be a true "separation of church and state." Jesus Himself will separate the sheep from the goats, the wheat from the tares, those who have been servants of God from those who have been servants of the devil—those who have served the Lord and those who have deserved punishment. On that Day the world will be forever torn from the midst of the Church.

Then Jesus pointed to four witnesses of His credibility:

1. He said that John the Baptist bore witness of Him, yet they refused to allow his burning and shining light to illuminate their hearts.

2. The signs that accompanied the ministry of Jesus attested to the fact that God was with Him. They bore witness that the Father sent Him.

3. The Scriptures testified of the coming Messiah, giving specific details of where He would be born, His lineage, His life and His death,

but still they were not willing to come to Him that they might have life.

4. Moses Himself wrote about Jesus. The very one they professed to honor said that a prophet would be raised up, like himself. But those who refused to listen to the Law would not allow it to be the school-master that it is, to bring them to Christ. If they didn't believe the writings of Moses, how would they believe the words of Jesus?

There is nothing new under the sun. Contemporary Jews still prefer their own traditions to Holy Scripture. In 1993, Jews in New York began Yom Kipper with a long blast of the ram's horn. Then began ten holy "days of awe." There is no mention of ten days of awe in scripture, so it would be therefore far more beneficial to them not have ten days of awe, but to look to the Ten Commandments which furnish awe in the hearts of those who see them in truth.

The president of the National Center for Learning and Leadership published a book which depicts the holy days as a trial—a type of Judgment Day. This will be a time when sinful man stands before the awesome and holy Creator of all things, from whose face the earth and heavens flee away. However, instead of falling on one's face in terror, the author says that as each person's trial takes place, "tension lightens and people relax enough to see that the Judge is not an impersonal authority who will be relentless, but rather, a loving old friend." So much for awe. Israel still clings to her idols.

Chapter Six
Supernatural Sandwiches

After these things, Jesus crossed the Sea of Galilee, presumably by boat, even though He had the unique option to walk across the sea. A great multitude followed Him, drawn by the signs He performed on the afflicted. Then He went up a mountain and sat down with His disciples.

It was near the time of the Passover, when the Jews celebrated the angel of death passing over those who applied the blood of the lamb to their door posts, so long ago in Egypt. As the Lamb of God sat with His disciples, He lifted up His eyes and looked upon the multitude, and asked Philip how they were going to be fed. Jesus already planned to perform a miracle, but Philip was earthly-minded and the supernatural realm wasn't an option. Andrew mentioned that a lad had five barley loaves and two small fish, but they were mere crumbs and small fries compared to such a large crowd.

So, Jesus instructed His disciples to have the assembly of 5,000 men sit down. He took the bread, gave thanks and distributed it to the disciples who took it and the fish to those who were seated, and everyone was filled.

The Bread of Life was breaking bread, which was symbolic of His body being broken for the life of the world. As each believer partakes in the bread, he in turn takes the Bread of Heaven to those who are dying for want of the Savior.

When all had eaten, the disciples gathered twelve baskets full of the fragments—one basket full for each disciple. God has a ministry for every disciple.

The miracle impressed the multitude to a point where they were about to take Jesus by force and make Him a king, so He departed from them and went up a mountain to be alone, because His "hour" had not yet come.

The disciples took conventional transport (they didn't yet have their sea-legs), but Jesus decided this time to walk across the sea . . . He created it, therefore it was beneath His feet.

As the disciples rowed their way through a storm, they saw a sight that dwarfed their fear of the tempest; Jesus walking towards them on the sea!

A kind word consoled their fears, and they willingly received Him into the boat.

Life itself can be a storm for the Christian. When we set on a course to do the will of God, a fearful hurricane breaks loose against us. It is the knowledge that all things are squarely and solely beneath the feet of Jesus, that gives us the good sense to let Him take hold of the helm of our ship. Suddenly, the storm seems of little consequence.

If the sea bows to His dictates, then every dirty and disgusting demon, every devastating difficulty, every dreadful danger, dilemma, disquiet, disaster, distress and even death itself will fall decidedly docile and dumb-founded before Him. We will, like the delighted and delivered disciples, find that the boat will then "immediately be at the land where we are heading."

If God is for us, nothing can be against us.

Hot Dog Hound

The common people were mystified as to what mode of transport Jesus took. Multitudes began to seek Him, and when they found Him, they asked for details. Jesus didn't answer their question, but informed them as to why they were seeking Him. They couldn't see beyond their stomachs. They liked the quality of the bread Jesus created when He fed the multitudes. They were carnal men and women, and therefore they lived only in the sensual realm.

I once spent some time witnessing to Leonard, a man in his late thirties. As I went through each of the Commandments, he looked deeply into my eyes. I could feel a sense of profound connection with his soul. I went through into Grace, labored the cross, spoke of God's love, the necessity of repentance, the danger of neglect, and the terrors of God's eternal Justice. He seemed to hang onto each word, all the while looking acutely and thoughtfully into my eyes. He then stared intently at me as if he was going to ask something of tremendous importance, and said, "I wonder if there's a hot dog stand around here."

I wasn't discouraged, in fact his words made me smile. My confidence was in the fact that the battle was the Lord's. I was merely sowing, but He would give the increase. The man was hungry, and like any carnal man, his stomach was more important to him than his eternal salvation. His god was his belly. It would take the Spirit of God to give him light as to his priorities, and that often takes time and instruction from the Word.

A Slice of Heaven

This is precisely what Jesus did with His fresh heavenly-bread-lovers. He told them not to put their energies into bread that perishes, but into the food that endures to everlasting life. Man doesn't live by bread alone, but by every word that proceeds from the mouth of God. He was referring to Himself. As the Word incarnate He was the life source that proceeded from the mouth of the Spirit of God.

When they seemed convinced by His words, and asked what they should do to do the will of the Father, He said that the work of God was to believe in the Son. Their next line was interesting. What would Jesus do next? Would He give them manna from Heaven as Moses gave their forefathers?

His listeners were Mosesites. They venerated Moses the miracle-worker when they should have given *God* the praise. God, not Moses gave them bread from Heaven, and it was this same God that had provided the Bread of Life who stood before them. Then Jesus made another reference to the cross.

He also made some more incredible statements:

1. He said that He was the Bread of Life.

2. He claimed to satisfy the hunger and thirst of all that believe on Him.

3. He claimed pre-existence.

4. He would not lose one who came to Him.

5. He would raise the dead on the "last day."

Once again, small-minded carnal men had small and carnal reactions to great spiritual truth. They murmured against Him because He said that He was the Bread who came down from Heaven.

That morsel stuck like dry bread in their camel-swallowing throats. Their reasoning minds began to rationalize the situation:

This was Jesus, whom they thought

to be the son of Joseph. They knew Joseph and Mary, the parents of this man, so it was ludicrous to say that He came down from Heaven!

The festering wound of reason had been opened. The next string of statements from Jesus would be salt that would sting with offence, or cleanse and cure. Faith would be the defining factor.

This man from Nazareth claimed that:

1. No one could come to Him, unless the Father drew him.

2. He was the sole means of resurrection.

3. Anyone whom God had taught would come to Him.

4. He was the only One who had ever seen God.

5. He who believed in Jesus had everlasting life.

6. He was the Bread of Life.

7. All who ate of Him will live forever.

8. He would give His flesh for the life of the world.

9. His flesh was food and His blood was drink.

10. He was the true bread which came down from Heaven.

This was too much to swallow. They could deal with the miracles, but this was getting bizarre—Jesus was speaking the language of cannibalism. Their faith in Him was consumed by their rationality.

When He knew that his disciples murmured about this, He said "Does this offend you?" What if they saw Him ascend back into Heaven? What if the sky was to open with great clouds, power and glory? What if all of creation, the angels in Heaven and God Himself attested to who Jesus was? Then they would abandon their reasoning minds and trust in Him.

The flesh doesn't have any profit; His words were spirit and life. He was no cannibal. He was making *spiritual* statements—speaking light to blind men. If His speech was in the literal realm, then He was bread, a door, a vine, a shepherd and His followers really were branches, lights and sheep who prayed in closets.

The ground in which they stood was one that could not receive truths of the Spirit of God. They sank into the quicksand of futile human reasoning.

Jesus knew those of His disciples that

were genuine and those who were false. True followers let faith in Him silence their reasoning. They trust in the Lord with all their heart and lean not to their own understanding. When He says that no one can come to Him unless it has been granted by the Father, it doesn't offend them as it did many of those who professed to be His disciples. They would rather face death, than turn their backs on Him who is the source of life. Where can Christians go if they turn against Jesus? There is no other name under Heaven given among men, whereby they can be saved. He alone—not Buddha, not Krishna, not the Pope, not the priest, not the Rabbi, not the pastor . . . He alone has the words of eternal life.

Not all the spurious believers left that day. There was one who stayed, thinking he had everyone fooled.

In 1989, when the mandatory use of seat belts went into effect in Italy, Dr. Claudio Ciaravolo (a psychiatrist from Naples) invented a white T-shirt with a diagonal black stripe. It was specifically designed to fool the police, so that they would think motorists were wearing their seat belts. *That's really clever.* He should also invent a T-shirt for fighter pilots, one that looks just like a parachute.

The world is full of people who think they have outwitted God. Their "T-shirt" will no doubt bring a great sense of joy for their own imaginative wit, until they have a head-on collision with Eternal Justice.

One stayed with the disciples when all others left. He had a vested interest in the ministry of Jesus of Nazareth. He was onto a good thing—Judas Iscariot had his sticky fingers in the money bag.

Chapter Seven
Family Faithlessness

When someone is wanting to kill you, it's not wise to go near them. Jesus didn't want to walk in Judea, because the Jews had murder on their minds.

Little is known about His brothers, but one can't help but wonder if there was not resentment towards this perfect sibling. How would you feel if your kid brother never did anything wrong? It was always you with rod indents on the hinderpart; it was always you with your nose in the corner . . . never Him.

When put to the test, his brethren wouldn't trust Him with their spiritual welfare, thinking He was out of His mind (Mark 3:21). They even encouraged Him to go back to Judea, but He said His hour was not yet come.

His hour was not yet come, but their hour and our hour is always ready and waiting. Jesus determined and knew the hour of his death, we don't.

He then gave insight as to why the Jews wanted to kill Him. He was hated merely because He spoke the truth. He testified of the world's deeds, that they were evil. He shone the flashlight of truth into the hidden and dark corners of the world's sinful heart. Those who side with the world, will be loved by the sin-loving world, and those who preach that sinners have sinned against God by violating His Law, will be hated by law-breakers.

University of Heaven

It's interesting to note that His brothers weren't altogether godless. They were committed enough to leave their homes and go to the Feast of Tabernacles, the Jewish feast which was held each year on the 15th day of the 7th month.

Even though Jesus attended the celebration incognito, He was the talk of the feast. The Jews sought to kill Him, but among the common people there was a great divergence of opinion about Him.

Some said He was good, others said He was a deceiver.

There was no middle ground in what we can believe about Him. Either He was or wasn't God in human form. Either He was good or bad. His teachings were either rooted in truth or in deception. Whatever their opinion, it was given in whispers because the people feared the Jews.

Suddenly, about the middle of the feast, Jesus appeared in the midst of the temple and began to teach with such eloquence and knowledge, He caused even His skeptics to marvel.

I once saw a painting in a restaurant in which a group of Chinese people were gathered around an elderly and grey-haired man. The painting was normal except for the old man's forehead. It was the size of a basketball. I suspected that it symbolized that he was a wise man, so I asked the woman who served us if my supposition was correct. When she told me that the man's head was swelled because of knowledge, I said that I knew quite a few university students just like that.

Knowledge however, didn't "puff up" Jesus. He said His doctrine wasn't His but God's, and if someone wanted to please God, he would know that Jesus spoke from the Father. He then affirmed

His own sinlessness, and began to use the Law to bring the knowledge of sin to Israel's sinful and adulterous generation. He told them that none of them kept the Law, and that if they professed to keep it, why was transgression of the Sixth Commandment burning in their hearts?

This was too much for the crowd. When they told Him He was nothing but a paranoid demoniac, He reminded them of the man He healed at the Sheep Gate and how they marveled, yet complained that He violated the Law Himself. He then showed them that their accusations were groundless. Their judgment of Him was superficial and erroneous.

Confused Doubters

It was known among the people that the Jews were trying to kill Him, but He was speaking boldly and no one was trying to stop Him. The Jews then began to show the shallow nature of their knowledge of the Scriptures. The Word of God made it abundantly clear where the Messiah would spring from, and even what He would say and do.

Jesus told them plainly that He was the Christ who had come down from Heaven to do the will of the Father. When He said, "But I know Him, for I am from

Him, and He sent Me," their blood boiled over, and they sought to lay hands on Him, but His hour had not yet come.

It seemed the time was right. The whole crowd had turned against Jesus, so the Pharisees and the chief priests sent officers to arrest Him, but the officers decided to listen to what He had to say before they apprehended Him. This is what they heard:

1. He was going back to God.

2. No one will be able to follow Him.

3. If anyone thirsted, they could drink from Him.

4. Rivers of living water would flow out of the hearts of those who believed in Him.

They watched the confusion and anger of those who doubted Him, and the excitement of those who believed. Some said He was a prophet, some that He was the promised Christ, while others showed their ignorance of His origins by thinking that He wasn't born in Bethlehem. Once again, the light brought division as it did in the beginning of creation.

It was then that the officers returned to the chief priests and the Pharisees, who asked why they were empty-handed.

Empty-handed they were, but empty-headed they were not.

Their explanation is most wonderful—"No man ever spoke like this man!"

These officers were witnesses to the gracious words that came from His mouth. This Man was different from the political zealots they had arrested in the past. He hadn't done anything that warranted His seizure. In fact, His words were like a light in darkness.

The Pharisees accused them of being deceived and appealed to their sense of reason. Had anyone with common sense and brain-power, any social standing, any leaders of Jewish society believed in Him? No, this was merely a leader of the cream of the scum of the cursed low class. From their high-browed seat of the scornful, they thought that those who didn't know the Law were cursed, when it is those who have knowledge of the Law, yet fail to obey it, that are the ones who are cursed. The more light, the more the guilt.

Suddenly, someone of the not so low class defended Jesus. Nicodemus, who had also witnessed gracious words from His mouth, pointed to the Law, saying that any accused person has a right to defend himself before being condemned

(Deuteronomy 1:16 17).

The Pharisees' attempts to justify their attitude shows how much they knew of the Scriptures. They said that no prophet had risen out of Galilee. Isaiah 9:1 proved them to be wrong.

Chapter Eight
Between a Rock and a Hard Place

Everyone went to his own house, but Jesus went to the Mount of Olives. He said Himself that foxes and birds had their own dwelling, but He had nowhere to rest His head. More than likely, He went there to pray. The next day, He went back to the temple and began an early morning Bible study.

It was during this meeting that the scribes and Pharisees thrust in front of Him a woman who had been caught in the act of adultery, and reminded Him that the Law of Moses demanded her death. They did this, not because they cared about justice, but because they had an ulterior motive. They wanted to find something of which to accuse Jesus.

They wanted to see Him transgress the Law by failing to uphold its perfect ordinances. They had infinitely more chance of finding an iceberg on the face of the sun.

Instead of defending the guilty woman, Jesus stooped down and wrote on the ground with His finger, as though He did not hear. He then raised Himself and said, "He who is without sin among you, let him throw a stone at her first."

It is ironic that here was the One who was without sin, yet instead of casting the stones of justice, He reached out the hand of mercy. Again, He stooped down and wrote on the ground.

I'm in good company when I suppose that Jesus wrote out the Ten Commandments. The reason for this is clear:

1. The Law was also written with the finger of God.

2. They were already conversing about the Law.

3. The Law "stops the mouth" (Romans 3:19), and that's what happened.

4. The Law stirs the conscience, and that's also what happened in this

incident.

5. Jesus wrote on the ground in two stages. The Law has two parts—the first four Commandments are vertical. They speak of man's responsibility to God, and the last six are horizontal, speaking of man's responsibility to man.

If it was the Law Jesus wrote with His finger, it is relevant that He wrote it in the sand. Had this woman been found in adultery under the Mosaic dispensation, when the Law was written in stone, her blood would have been spilled under its wrath. The Law in stone was hard and merciless, but because she was found in transgression at the feet of the Savior, the sea of mercy could wash away that same Law written in sand. This wasn't the sea of compromise, because the water was stained crimson with the blood of the Messiah.

On seeing what Jesus wrote and hearing His words, they began to leave, beginning at the eldest, until no one was left except Jesus and the woman. When there were no accusers, she was told to go, and to sin no more.

What a fearful thing it is when we face God's Law. The very stones call for our blood. The Law cries out for justice. It has no mercy. Its demand is, "The soul that sins shall die!" But the Judge who rules can, at His own discretion, administer the *spirit* of the Law, and its spirit says that mercy rejoices over judgment—God is rich in mercy to all that call upon Him.

The letter kills, but the Spirit brings life. God is not willing that the wrath of the Law fall upon guilty sinners, because He would rather acquit the criminal from the courtroom . . . and He can do so because of Calvary.

It was A.N. Martin who said,

"The moment God's Law ceases to be the most powerful factor in influencing the moral sensitivity of any individual or nation, there will be indifference to Divine wrath, and when indifference comes it always brings in its train indifference to salvation."

When a nation turns its back on Divine Law, it pulls up anchor in a storm. It drifts aimlessly towards the rocks of anarchy. Even the world loses respect for civil law when it no longer stands for that which is just and right. On October 29, 1988, a man in New York stabbed his ex-wife eleven times with a kitchen knife. The woman recovered from her horrific wounds, including one that destroyed her voice box.

Her ex-husband was sentenced to 25 years in prison, but from prison filed a law-suit over the validity of their 1985 divorce. The actions cost his ex-wife $7,000 to defend herself, while his legal fees, because he had a court-appointed lawyer, didn't cost him a dime.

The average life term given to murderers in the U.S. is 15 years. The average term served by murderers is just over 5 years. Each year in the United States over 24,000 people are murdered.

However, the Law of God in Israel still had a lethal bite to it. Adulterers were to be stoned to death, and that ordinance banished indifference from the adulterous woman. It stopped her mouth, and opened her sinful heart to the Grace of God in Christ.

She was left *alone* at the feet of the Savior of the world; and when the exposed sinner stands before the Lord, guilty and undone, it is nobody else's business. Jesus deals with us in private. The tabloids could have a hundred headlines, and sell a million papers if each of our secret sins were made known, but the night I stood before the Savior, it was just me and Jesus—and He cast my sins into the sea of His forgetfulness. All He asks is that we go our way and sin no more.

Christians who have stood under the shadow of the ten great rocks of the Law, hear a little more than "sin no more." They remember His sobering words to the blind man He healed, when He said, "Lest a worse thing come upon you." The Christian knows that the earthly consequence of sin can be disease and suffering, but they also understand that a *worse* thing will come upon those who are found guilty on the Day of Wrath.

They no longer walk in darkness. They fear Him who can cast both body and soul into Hell, and they follow close to Him who is the light of the world.

Their eyes are ever towards Jesus, and any dark shadows cast by their life are merely in their wake.

Some time after the incident with the sinful woman, Jesus spoke about being the light of the world, and the Pharisees once again revealed their ignorance. They began to accuse Him of being a false prophet, but He reiterated that He spoke the truth and that His Father sent Him, saying that they neither knew Him nor the Father.

How confusing for the conceited Pharisees. Jesus was still speaking strange words, but this time it wasn't to His mother whose trust in Him kept her from being perplexed. He told them:

1. He was going to depart.

2. They would try and find Him.

3. They will die in their sin.

4. They could not follow Him.

5. They were from beneath, He was from above.

6. They were of this world, He was not of this world.

7. That their state of righteousness depended entirely upon their acceptance of Him.

8. He had many things to say and judge concerning them.

9. When they "lifted" Him up, they would know He was the Messiah.

10. Everything He did and said came from the Father.

He then said something no other human being has been able to say. He said that He always did those things that pleased God. Here was a Man who was weighed in the balance and not found "wanting." The scales of Eternal Justice didn't tip when they balanced the life of Jesus of Nazareth. Not once did He transgress the perfect, good, holy and just Law of God, either in thought, word or deed. Here is the "man" of Psalm One, who walked not in the counsel of the ungodly, nor stood in the way of sinners, nor sat in the seat of the scornful.

This Man delighted in and meditated on the Law of God both day and night. He was the One who may abide in God's tabernacle and dwell in His holy hill, because He walked uprightly and worked righteousness in His heart. He had clean hands and a pure heart.

He was the Good Samaritan who picked us up on the road to Jericho, poured the oil of His Spirit and the wine of His love into the wounds of our sin, and carried us to the Inn of God's care, promising to supply our every need until He comes back.

The Law's demand to love God with heart, mind, soul, and strength, and to love our neighbor as much as one's self, was satisfied in Him and in Him alone.

Jesus then told His many followers that they needed to prove themselves by continuing in His word, and the fruit of obedience would be a knowledge of the truth that would make them free.

Naturally, the Jews took what He said naturally and said they were already free. He then said, "Whoever commits sin is a slave to sin," something the world would argue with vehemently, until it gave the thought some thought.

Let's look at just a few contemporary sins: cleptomania, over-eating, alcoholism, and pornography. Cleptomania is a pleasant word for uncontrollable theft. This is treated as a disease because the person cannot help but "shop-lift." They need special "treatment." In other words they are slaves to the sin of theft.

Soul Control

Sympathize though we may with people given to obesity, their problem is no more than a lack of self-control. They have lost control of their will. They have become slaves to their sin, their god has become their belly. The Scriptures say that the "righteous shall eat to the satisfying of his soul." If you are godly, you will practice temperance, something the world laughs at. You will restrain your appetite for food. You may even fast to bring your craving for edibles under the control of your will. What this will do is make you truly thankful for your food when you do eat, and you will be satisfied with less on your plate.

The obese however, are never satisfied. The unbridled and unbroken stallion of lust for food has bucked them out of the saddle. They no longer hold the reins; they have no say in how much they eat, and they eat until they vomit, and still go back for more.

The righteous eats *to the satisfying of his soul*. When he has finished his plate of food, it is his *soul*, not his body which should have been in control. When he pulls his appetite to a grinding halt, it stops in its tracks. His appetite takes the back seat, and his will grips a firm hold of the reins. In fact, Jesus said that we were to cut our hand off, or pluck our eye out if the body offended God and therefore hindered our eternal welfare. The salvation of the soul should always take priority over the salivation of the body. This is why Solomon said that if I was given to appetite, I should put a knife to my throat.

We are told alcoholism is a disease, when God says drunkenness is a sin (1 Corinthians 6:10). Alcoholics are sad and pathetic slaves of sin.

When the world establishes special

"treatment" centers for people who have problems with pornography, they are merely bearing witness to the words of the Savior, "Whoever commits sin is a slave to sin," but those whom the Son sets free, are free indeed, and that freedom comes only through discipline (John 8:31-32). Jesus knew that those to whom He was speaking were Abraham's seed, but He also knew that they wanted to kill Him. If they were truly the children of Abraham, they would do the works of Abraham.

He told them that they did the *deeds* of their father, and they reacted by saying that they weren't born in fornication because *God* was their Father. Their response revealed that the word "Father" wasn't the thing that irritated them, but the word "deeds." When Jesus said "*father*," He used the word "pater," the same word they used when they said God was their Father. Their answer showed that they knew that their deeds were not harmonious with the God they professed to call "Father."

Cheese Rejection

If I give you a small slice of cheese from a large block (the taste being constant throughout the whole block), and you spit the cheese out saying you hate the taste, then you reject the whole block. Jesus was God manifest in human form. If the Jews rejected Him, they rejected the Father—he who is of God hears God's words. John later stated in his epistle " . . . everyone that loves Him loves Him also that is begotten of Him" (1 John 5:1).

Then came the supreme insult: "You are of your father the devil, and the desires of your father you want to do." This must have made their blood boil. If you tell a godless person that the devil is their father, you may end up nursing a rearranged face, but here Jesus is telling the most "holy" of humanity, the mint and rue tithers, the praying, fasting, clean on the outside, robe-wearing religious leaders of the day, that they were from Hell itself!

Our *Real* Father

My friend and pastor, Garry Andsell was once an atheist. Not long after he was married, he decided he disliked children and had a vasectomy.

A few years later he was converted and immediately loved children. A reversal vasectomy failed, so at the age of 40 years, he and his wife Denise, adopted three children, two boys and a girl. They showered their love on these children like a burst dam of affection, which had been held back for the many years they couldn't have kids.

One day, when Garry told his six-year-old daughter that she couldn't do something she had set her heart on, she turned to him and said, "My *real* father would let me do it!"

When I heard of this incident, I remember thinking how difficult this must have been; how did he handle it? This is what he did. He told her the truth about her "real" father—that he was a loser, who was an adulterer and a liar. Then he pointed to the door and said, "There's the door, go to your real dad if you want to." The six-year-old cried, *"I'm sorry daddy,"* and rushed into his arms.

Sometimes, there is a temptation in the heart of God's adopted children to think that things would be better for us if we were in the world. The green grass on the other side of the fence looks soft and luscious, and deep in our wicked hearts we whisper, "My *real* father would let me do it." It is then that the Word of God says simply that our real father is the devil . . . the ultimate loser, the liar "from the beginning," who came to "kill, steal and destroy" (1 John 3:8-10).

God doesn't hold His children hostage. The door to Hell is there if we want to follow the devil and his angels. Good sense makes the child of God rush back to his Heavenly Father's arms and say, *"Abba, Father . . . I'm sorry!"*

Who I AM Is

The Pharisees then said the nastiest, offensive and most vicious thing they could think of as a come-back. They told Jesus that He was a Samaritan; that as far as they were concerned He was a half-breed, and they added one more little point—He had a demon.

How forgiving and gracious was the Son of God! I would have burned their tails with a lightning bolt, and laughed as they ran down the street towards the Pool of Siloam. But all Jesus did was deny it, saying that He honored His Father, they dishonored Him, and that if anyone kept His word, he would never see death. That confirmed their thought that He was demon-possessed.

Again they asked Him who He was and again Jesus told them, saying, "Your father Abraham rejoiced to see My day."

When Moses was told by God to tell the children of Israel that He was going to deliver them from Egypt by His hand, he asked what he should say when they asked, "What is His name?" God said to Moses,

> "'I AM WHO I AM.' Thus you shall say to the children of Israel, `I AM has sent me to you.'"

When Jesus said that Abraham rejoiced to see His day, the Jews surmised that there was no way that could have happened. Then came goose-bump generating words from this Man from Nazareth. He said, "Before Abraham was, I AM." If they were confused about what Jesus was saying in the past, now it became abundantly clear. He was claiming to be I AM! This was unthinkable— the ultimate, supreme and utmost profane and sacrilegious blasphemy, worthy of death by stoning . . . that is, unless it was true.

Chapter Nine
Eye Wash

It is merely human reasoning to presume that God blesses us with good things when we are good, and punishes us with bad things when we are bad.

That's why the disciples asked if a blind man or his parents had sinned to cause his condition. It was obviously bad karma.

Jesus said that it was neither caused by his or his parents' sins. If someone must be blamed, it is Adam:

> "Through one man sin entered the world, and death through sin, and thus death spread to all men, because all sinned" (Romans 5:12).

Death and the sufferings that issued from it came through our first father, but God doesn't punish the children for the sins of the fathers (Jeremiah 31:29-30), and if He did treat us according to our sins, we wouldn't live long enough to enjoy the blessings even a blind man enjoys.

Jesus then spoke of the urgency of His charge, and said again that He was the light of the world. He spat on the ground, made clay with the saliva, put it on the blind man's eyes, and told him to wash in the pool of Siloam.

Why did Jesus go to the trouble of putting clay on the man's blind eyes? He didn't *need* the clay—at His whisper the whole of blind humanity could receive sight, so why did He employ clay *as a prelude* to the healing of this man's eyes? Obviously, there is more here than meets the eye.

There is the thought that it was a test of the blind man's humility and obedience—a type of salvation for blind humanity. Like Naaman the leper, who was told to wash seven times in the muddy Jordan, he had to trust and obey before deliverance from leprosy came.

Think of the situation for a moment. The blind man was standing before the healer from Nazareth. His heart raced in anticipation. Perhaps he had heard about the healing of blind Bartimaeus.

Scripture tells us that Jesus did innumerable miracles which aren't recorded in the Bible. His fame spread like tabloid wildfire across Israel, so no doubt the man had heard about this miracle worker.

Faith in Jesus seemed to burst within the blind man's breast. What would this Jesus do? Would He say, "Your faith has made you whole," and suddenly light he had only heard about would flood his darkened soul? Or should he say, "Jesus, Son of David, have mercy on me!"? Would this Man reach out and actually touch his sightless eyes?

Perhaps as he waited, he heard a spitting sound and whispered to someone who stood by, "What's He doing?" The blind man winced just a little as the answer came that Jesus had spat on the clay. But, there are many things in life that leave a bad taste in one's mouth, so who doesn't spit once in a while?

As he waited, he whispered again to his friend, "What's He doing now?" The answer came, "He's making a mud-ball with the spit." The blind man looked a little concerned. His friend continued, "Now He's picking up the mud-ball and breaking it in two."

As the blind man mumbled, "*What's He*

doing n..!!" he was stopped from finishing his sentence, as he felt wet, cold mud on his eyes.

Think for a moment of how most of us would react in a similar situation. Didn't this merit offence? Wouldn't the man be justified in saying, "Making mud-balls with His spit is weird, but how dare He then put it on my eyes! *Is this some kind of twisted joke?* Is the crowd having a good chuckle? This is humiliating. I'm a *blind* man, *where is His compassion!"*

Instead, he humbly listened to the Master, then ran to do as He said. Like Naaman, He had faith, humility and obedience. He exercised the three necessary virtues we need to be saved, and his experience is obviously symbolic of salvation. Also like Naaman, he had no other hope. He was born blind, and had nothing to lose but his pride. So it is with the world.

Another thought is that Jesus may have done that which He did in the beginning, when He created Adam's eyes from the dust of the earth (Genesis 2:7). The Hebrew word used is "aphar" which means *clay*. He may have created new eyes for the blind man.

There is yet another thought. It was the mud that *compelled* the man to go to the pool to be cleansed. He had no *motivation* to go to the water to wash until Jesus put clay on his eyes. Imagine if Jesus had simply said, "Go to the pool of Siloam and wash." The man may have reacted by saying, *"But I'm not dirty, Lord."* Once he was aware of his uncleanness, he went without question.

It is when we apply the two tablets of God's Law to the darkened understanding of the sinner, that he has an inducement to go to the cleansing of the Gospel. Until he understands his uncleanness, he has no *reason* to go to the water of the blood of Christ. When the Law is pressed against his blinded eyes, he becomes aware that he is soiled and that all his righteous deeds are as filthy rags in the sight of God. The Law *compels* him to go to the Savior, it *necessitates* his cleansing—it is a "schoolmaster" to bring him to Christ.

Charles Spurgeon said,

"No man will ever put on the robe of Christ's righteousness till he is stripped of his fig leaves, nor will he wash in the fount of mercy till he perceives his filthiness. Therefore my brethren, we must not cease to declare the Law, its demands, its threatenings, and the sinner's multiplied breaches of it."

The hymn-writer had no desire to wash in the cleansing blood of the Savior, until the Law of God compelled him to do so:

> "By God's Word at last my sin I learned; then I trembled at the Law I'd spurned, 'til my guilty soul imploring turned, to Calvary."

The "laver" in the tabernacle was made of mirrors, and therefore would have given a true reflection of the state of those who were about to wash (Exodus 38:8). As the unregenerate "look into the perfect Law of Liberty" (James 1:25), it reveals their sin to them and shows them their want of cleansing.

You and I should never divide Jesus from the Law which was written on His heart (Psalm 40:7-8). The Scriptures predict that He would "magnify the Law and make it honorable" (Isaiah 42:21). That means that He would proudly promote its excellence. It is clear why He needed to do that. God's Law had been negated in the days of His flesh, and nowadays made void, both outside and inside of the Church. In our ignorance, we have failed to see that the Law is the expression of God's nature, His character, His very personality.

The Law Is the mind of God expressed to man, and if we scorn the Law, we are reproaching God, from whose hand it came.

Why did Jesus say He was the light of the world, before He applied clay to the man's eyes? It was because He was about to give the man light. He was going to give the man a bearing in his darkness, *before* he was healed. The Law is a beam of light from the lighthouse, in the storm of God's wrath. It directs him to the shelter of the cove of safety in Christ. Martin Luther said,

> "It is impossible for them (proud sinners) to know their sin. Therefore also they are not amenable to instruction. If they would know the Law, they would also know their sin; and sin to which they are now dead would become alive to them."

The Scent of Duty

The blind man found his sight at the pool of Siloam, which is an obvious "type" of the good news that we can be washed by the Savior's blood. Siloam means "sent," and it is a sad testimony to humanity that there needed to be a "Great Commission" given to the Church (Mark 16:15). *There shouldn't have to have been one.* Would a blind man need to be especially "sent" to tell people he has been healed? Should a man who has found bread *have* to be commissioned to take the excess to the starving? Andrew *found* Peter and brought him to Jesus, he didn't have to be sent. Philip *found* Nathanael and brought him to the Savior. Both of them went before they were sent, and conscience should send us with the Gospel, without having to be coerced by the Great Commission. The love of Christ should constrain us.

The blind man washed his eyes and was miraculously healed. What an amazing thing to witness. He was *born* blind! Can you imagine him staring in unbelief at the shimmering light in the pool as it danced on the water? Can you see tears form in his once blind eyes, as he perceives light for the first time in his life, and realizes the actuality of what is happening to him? Can't you hear him whisper, "I can see, *I can see!*" and become louder and louder as he runs his hands through the water, staring at the wet palms of his hands shouting, "I can see!"

Seeing such an incredible thing take place would be enough to bring a tear of inexpressible joy to the hardest of hearts; but not the hypocritical heart of a Pharisee. Dead religion is built from hearts of stone, which become tombstone walls between themselves and the God they profess to serve

The healed man was taken to the religious leaders, but instead of rejoicing at the miracle he experienced, they began to interrogate him. When they asked him how he had received his sight, he plainly told them. Some said that in healing him on the Sabbath, Jesus broke the Law, others disagreed. Again, light divided the darkness.

The man's parents were called in and questioned about their son. They said he was born blind, but sent the inquisitors back to their son because they valued their seat in the synagogue.

The Jews found the man and subtly said, "Give God the glory! We know that this man is a sinner." They tried to pressure him into feeling that to give God honor, he must discredit the very One who gave him sight. How could he do such a thing!

He merely said the undeniable: "Whether He is a sinner or not I do not know. One thing I know: once I was blind, but now I see."

When your eyes are opened by the touch of Jesus, expect an inquisition from an unbelieving world. They don't understand what happens because their own minds are blinded by the god of this world (2 Corinthians 4:4). If they did believe, then the light of the glorious Gospel of Christ who is the image of God would shine on them also.

We tell the world good tidings that make the blind man's healing fade into nothingness—we have found everlasting life in Jesus Christ! *We have found the unspeakable—the answer to the dilemma of death!* What is their reaction to the good news of the Gospel?—"How did He open your eyes? Jesus couldn't have done it because there are hypocrites in the Church . . . the Bible is full of mistakes . . . Where did Cain get his wife? . . . I don't need Jesus because I'm a good person . . . man came from apes!" Nuts.

As a new believer, you can't give appropriate defence to their objections, but one thing you do know—once you were blind but now you see! The person with an experience is never at the mercy of a person with an argument.

Again, the gnat-swallowing blind and ignorant guides asked him how his eyes were opened. He said that he had already told them, and no doubt with a smile in his new-found eye responded with, "Do you also want to be His disciples?" The Pharisees reacted in revulsion and spat out that they were *Moses* disciples, saying that they knew that God spoke to him, but they didn't even know where this . . . was from. The word "fellow" (which is in italics in scripture) isn't in the original language, and read without it, shows the disdain they had for Jesus. The Apostle Paul was so despised by the Jews and others that he was given the same scorn in Acts 18:13, 22:22 and 24:5, where he was called "A mover of sedition, a pestilent `fellow,' a ring-leader of a sect among the Jews."

When a young man once fell asleep during a lecture in Bible college, someone whispered in his ear, "You've been asked to close in prayer!" The youth immediately stood to his feet and closed the session, *right in the middle of the lecture.*

The Pharisees were asleep in the lecture. The very Teacher of Israel stood right in their midst and they didn't have a clue what was going on. When the man answered them, he revealed that more than his physical eyes were opened by Jesus; he seems to be speaking by the Spirit of God. His words are strong, gracious and full of truth, saying that what happened to him was a wonderful thing—that Jesus opened the eyes of a man *born* blind, and that if God hadn't been with Him, He could do nothing. Such light from a mere "sinner" was too much for his hearers, so they gave him the left foot of fellowship.

The statement of disdain used by the Pharisees "You were altogether born in sins" is a revealing one. It showed the misunderstanding the Pharisees had of the qualities of God, and of the true nature of sin.

I was once talking to a man about the fact that he had broken the Ten Commandments. He admitted that he had lied, stolen, and broken the Seventh Commandment through lust. His eyes suddenly lit up as he thought he had found a bush to hide behind. He said, "If God is good, as you say He is, then He will overlook my transgressions." I replied, "Imagine you are standing before a judge, guilty of killing someone while driving drunk at 80 m.p.h. The evidence is in and you have been found to be thoroughly guilty.

The judge looks directly at you and says, "Have you anything to say before I pass sentence?" You reply, "Your honor, I admit my transgression, but I take great confidence in the fact that you are a good man." The judge responds, "Yes, I am a good man *and because of that,* I will also be just."

The very fact that God is good, necessitates that He must therefore be honorable and just and punish sinners for transgression of His Law. Those who hope to hide behind the bush of God's goodness as a means to escape His justice, will find on the Day of Judgment that they will be flushed out with the fires of His consuming holiness.

Man, Prophet and God

Jesus then found the excommunicated man and asked him if he believed in the Son of God. When he enquired as to who the Son of God was, Jesus revealed that He was referring to Himself. He said, "You have both seen Him and it is He who is talking to you." The word Jesus used for see is *horao*, and means "to discern clearly . . . to experience." Earlier, when the healed man told the Pharisees that he could see, the word was *blepo*, which means "to behold, to look." Now the man knew that Jesus was more than a teacher, a healer, or a prophet, and the Bible says he said, "Lord, I believe!" and he worshipped Him.

Notice the awakening that came to the

once blind man. It has been rightly pointed out that he first saw the Lord as "a man called Jesus." Then he saw Him as a prophet, then one as a "worshipper of God and One who does His will," and finally, once he understood who Jesus really was, he worshipped Him.

How did the man "worship" Jesus? Did he prostrate himself, or did he kneel before Him? We are not given details, but the word comes from two English words "worth-ship," and is *proskuneo* in the Greek, meaning "to kiss, like a dog licking his master's hand." Only those who have had a faithful dog will truly appreciate the meaning.

Sometimes, I will begin a conversation with Sue, and see my dog gazing at me with the utmost admiration. Twenty minutes later, I look over at the dog, and she is still staring at me with a star-struck expression. This happens almost daily (with the dog and Sue).

The servant of Jesus Christ gazes with the utmost admiration towards the Master. One word from Him and he runs to do His will. He lives for His smile.

Chapter Ten
Who Is Ivis Presley?

Hundreds of years earlier, David had written that the Lord was his shepherd, and now that shepherd had become flesh. Here is a continuance of the most famous of Psalms, Psalm 23. This was the "Great Shepherd" Himself (Hebrews 13:20); the One who takes away the "want" of the covetous human heart. He was the path of righteousness, who brought light to the valley of the shadow of death. Here was the Bread of Life, placed by God on a table in the presence of our enemies. Heaven's cup "ran over," and brought the Father's goodness and mercy to us, so that we might dwell in the House of the Lord forever.

God's Word says that a good shepherd is one who feeds the sheep with "knowledge and understanding" (Jeremiah

3:15). Jesus qualified as the Good Shepherd—Isaiah 53:11 tells us that by the knowledge of the Messiah many would be justified, and the New Testament says that the Son of God has come and given us understanding (1 John 5:20).

There are many who seek to "dwell in the House of the Lord forever," but they will not if they do not enter by the Door. Jesus was the first to enter the door. It was opened to Him by His Father, and all that come after Him will hear His voice and follow Him. They are not hearers of the Word only, therefore they put legs to their ears. The reason that they follow Him is that they know His voice and trust Him with their souls. His voice is the sound of genuine love. In fact, evidence that we have entered through the door will be that we know His voice (John 10: 3-5,16).

The sheep-fold in Bible times was a rectangled area surrounded by a wall and a doorway. The wall was protected at the top by a layer of thorns, safeguarding the flock from predators. God's hand of care is forever over His children. The soul of the Christian will never perish; no one will pluck it from the Father's hand.

When Jesus used His usual parabolic language, His hearers were baffled once again, so He told them plainly that He was the door of the sheep and that all those who came before Him claiming to be the Christ, the Messiah, or someone special, were but thieves and robbers, and that those who loved the truth did not follow them.

True believers are likened to sheep, which:

1. Are easily led (they submit without resistance).

2. Flock together (in unity).

3. Need a shepherd (or they stray).

4. Imitate one another.

5. Are productive (wool, meat, leather and milk)

6. Were used in sacrifice.

7. Were a sign of God's blessing.

8. Were also a type of Israel (Matthew 10:6).

9. Were a sign of God's blessing (Deuteronomy 7:13).

10. Will be divided from the "goats" at the Judgment

The symbolism is clear. There are many voices coming from "false prophets in sheep's clothing," therefore we must learn the voice of the Good Shepherd so that we won't be led astray. We must flock together, not forsaking the assembling of ourselves together as is the manner of some. We need to follow Jesus, because without Him we are sheep going astray, turning "everyone to his own way." We are to be "imitators" of Paul, as he was of Christ. We must be productive, always laboring in the Lord, for we know that our labor is not in vain.

We are to present ourselves as living sacrifices, holy and acceptable unto the Lord, which is our reasonable service, knowing that day will come when the Church will be transformed, glorified in a moment, in the twinkling of an eye, revealing the richness of God's blessing on the Church.

Finally, a Christian should always keep the knowledge of the great and terrible Day of the Lord in the forefront of his mind, when the Good Shepherd divides those who served God and those who served the devil.

This will furnish a healthy fear of God, which will keep him from sin.

Steals & Deals

Jesus then contrasted Himself with the devil (the "d" is optional). He called him a thief who came to not only steal, but to kill and then destroy. This is what he did in the garden of Eden.

He stole Adam's eternal happiness; he killed him, and if it wasn't for the Grace of God, he would have completely destroyed the entire adamic offspring.

Friends of ours once purchased a cane for their father, but when they gave it to him, they saw a label which said, "Judas stick," and therefore threw it away (even though they didn't know what a "Judas stick" was). I told them that when sheep are being led to the slaughter, they often follow a "Judas" sheep up a ramp. Just before the Judas sheep passes through the death door, it is separated so that it can continue to lead others to their death. The Judas stick was probably used to separate the Judas from the rest of the sheep.

There are men who stand in pulpits nowadays and use the rod of authority for the devil rather than for God. They are (often unwittingly) tools of satan to lead sinners into a false conversion—one that seems to be genuine, but lacks the proclamation of the whole counsel of God. Their rod is not the rod of God, but a betrayal of the cause of the Gospel.

Jesus didn't come to kill, steal and destroy, He came to make alive, to give, and to save. His mission was to bring life to the world, both quantitative and qualitative. He is the Good Shepherd, who came to give His life for the sheep, and that is the difference between the true and false shepherd. A "hireling" (one who is hired for money), thinks only of his own welfare, not the welfare of his sheep. He leaves when tribulation comes, because he serves mammon rather than God.

Jesus then spoke of "other sheep," an obvious reference to the Gentiles who would enter the Kingdom of God after Israel had her opportunity (Isaiah 56:8). When she despised the Gospel, the Apostle Paul said,

"Therefore let it be known to you that the salvation of God has been sent to the Gentiles, and they will hear it!" (Acts 28:28).

When the Messiah was crucified, He wasn't "murdered" in the normal understanding of the word, neither did He commit suicide as some have surmised. His life was not taken from Him, neither did He take it Himself. He *gave* it. He gave it because it was in the plan of the Father to redeem the world through the sacrificial Lamb; God was in Christ, reconciling the world to Himself.

Look at His remarkable words: "I have power to lay it down, and I have power to take it again."

Only God could speak in such a way. Death was to Him but a tiny and dry leaf in the way of a mammoth hurricane.

These sayings were too hard to reconcile with the fact that this was an ordinary man, a carpenter from Nazareth. So, those who didn't accept His deity, continued to say that He was demonically-controlled, and tried to dissuade ones from listening to His words. Others were not so self-deceptive and reasoned that a man who is possessed by evil doesn't go about doing good, healing those who were born blind.

The Light in the Porch

It was the Feast of Dedication (the Feast of "Hanukkah" is still celebrated by the Jews today), and as Jesus walked openly in the Temple in Solomon's porch, the Jews surrounded Him and questioned Him as to who He was. Again, He affirmed that He was the Christ, saying that the miracles that issued from His hands were sign enough for them to believe, but they didn't believe because they were not of His sheep.

He told them that He was the giver of eternal life, and all those who came to Him would have assurance that no man would separate them from His, nor from His Father's hand.

No doubt, calling God His "Father" again stirred a spirit of murder, but then came, "I and My Father are one." That caused them to take stones in their eager hands to stone Him to death, but He stopped them with His words—*for which work were they about to stone Him*? They replied, that they weren't about to stone Him for His good works, but for the blasphemy of saying that He was God.

Then Jesus confounded them with a verse of Scripture that still confounds many today. He told them that they were "gods." The word in Hebrew is *elohiym*, and, although it does mean "gods," it can also be interpreted to mean "judges." It was a direct quote from Psalm 82:6, and in its context it would seem to be a reference to the fact that God had given the leaders of Israel authority to exercise judgment (verses 1,2 & 8). If God so honored the sons of Adam by using the word *elohiym* to describe those who would "die like men," why were they so offended and claimed He was a blasphemer, when God had sanctified the Son and sent Him into the world?

God the Father sent the Son, yet they still would not believe. He confirmed that His hand was with Him by mighty signs and wonders, but still they didn't believe.

Here we see the love of Christ displayed. He urged these proud, self-righteous hypocrites to "believe the works, that you may know and believe that the father is in Me, and I in Him." He was deeply interested in their eternal welfare, despite their hypocrisy and wilful ignorance. Thank God for His patience, because many of us were just like the blind leaders of the blind. We ourselves were once foolish, disobedient and deceived (Titus 3:3).

Sinners often delude themselves. They live a lie. I was once speaking to a young man called Paul who typified this. As I reasoned with him about Judgment Day and the fact he had broken God's Law, I mentioned the subject of premarital sex. He asked, *"Is that wrong?"* Oh dear. Here was a poor man whom God had left with no knowledge of right and wrong. *Sure.* I told him it was wrong, and that "fornicators" would not inherit the Kingdom of God. He shuffled in his seat.

He then asked, "Is it wrong to drive without a license?" More sweet innocence. I told him that God commanded us to obey the laws of the land. More shuffling. He looked down at his CD player and said, "I think this was stolen when I bought it. I only paid $30, and it's worth about $90." I said, "You've received stolen goods, so you're a thief."

He looked at me and said, *"I didn't know."* I said, "Yes you did, and you're in big trouble." He said, "Sometimes, when I'm alone in the dark I get scared, but when I've done something good, I feel O.K." I told him that he was like Adam running from God when he sinned against Him.

I said that if he had just stolen a car and I was a police officer, he would be fearful, *because he was a law-breaker*.

The truth of the matter is that his own heart told him sex out of marriage, driving without a license and receiving stolen goods were wrong, but his love for sin deluded him to the fact of divine retribution.

Too Close For Comfort

A number of years ago, I drove my car along a driveway and saw a strange word written in bold white paint on the pavement parallel to the road. The word read "IOMPH." I remember mouthing the strange word in a whisper as I puzzled over what it meant—"I-UMF?" Suddenly, I felt stupid as I realized it was telling what speed I should be driving!

More recently, I stood in line at a Post Office and stared at a curious poster. It was strange because it spoke of some guy called Ivis Presley. I thought, "Who on earth is *Ivis* Presley?" Directly after his name, there were more names—Otis Redding, Buddy Holly. I had heard of those guys, but never of Ivi . . . Suddenly, I saw a large "E" in a different style print and color in front of Ivis's name. The word was actually "Elvis," not *Ivis*.

My problem with both of these humbling experiences, was that I was too close to the forest to see the trees. The obvious was right in front of me, I hadn't seen it. I needed to pull back a little and just exercise a little thought. That was also the problem with the Pharisees. The Messiah, the very One their precious Scriptures wrote about, stood right in front of them, yet they did not see Him.

However, a number did pull back a little, and give some deep thought to the fact that undeniable miracles emanated from this Man, and believed in Him because of the signs, saying that everything John the Baptist said about Him was true.

Chapter Eleven
When He Who Snoozes Wins

There was sickness in the family of Mary and Martha. It was serious enough for the sisters to send a message to Jesus, saying that he whom He loved was sick. The message made clear the mandate for Jesus. If He loved Lazarus, He would immediately respond to the message and come and heal him. This was the same Mary who at the house of Simon the Leper, had poured a very costly oil upon Jesus and wiped His feet with her hair. She was one whose love for the Son of God was evident, so surely He would instantly respond to her request.

Scripture tells us that Jesus *did* love Mary, Martha and Lazarus, yet He stayed where He was for two days. He said that the sickness had a purpose, that it was for the glory of God, and that the Son of God would be glorified through it.

Jesus knew that Lazarus was dying. He had the power to save him from death, yet He did nothing.

The ways of God are infinitely above the ways of man. Two years before my conversion, Sue and I owned a surf shop. The shop was also an outlet for leather jackets and suede coats I custom-made for people. After I became a Christian, I dropped to my knees and gave God my business, saying, "Lord, it's Yours completely." A month later, a large gentleman walked into the building and said, "I have just bought this property. I want you out of here within a month." I had no lease, so I abandoned the surfing side, and began manufacturing jackets and coats at home.

A short time later, a member of the local council came around home and informed me that I was breaking a bylaw by having a commercial sewing machine in a residential area. I had to move once again.

I prayed for somewhere to set up my machine in the commercial area, but it seemed the heavens were as brass; I couldn't find even one square yard. Much to my dismay, I was forced to open a store six miles away, in the heart of the city.

Now that I look back, I can see that what seemed to be God ignoring me, was actually His hand guiding me. Had I not moved into the city, I would never have begun public speaking in the local square, something I did almost daily for twelve years, giving me experience which later led into a full-time itinerant ministry.

This incident with Lazarus shows us that God can have a hand, even in what seems to be the ultimate adversity.

When Jesus said that He was going to Judea, His disciples were immediately concerned for His safety, but he told them in His way that He knew what He was doing by saying, "Are there not twelve hours in the day?" The Jewish day was from morning to evening, while the night was divided into "watches." Only those who are in darkness, stumble.

He then revealed His knowledge of Mary and Martha's situation. He knew very well that after the two day wait Lazarus was now dead, yet He referred to death as a sleep from which He would awaken him.

The world finds moments of joy in this transient and pain-filled life. Joy wells up through the heart when a woman holds her first child, or a man gets a "hole in one," or a surfer finds a perfect wave. They experience what is called en-joy-ment. But the Christian has joy *unspeakable*. The joy he has is indescribable. The world's joy becomes but a memory, while the Christian's bliss comes from what will be. He has a hope which is both sure and steadfast, an anchor of the soul.

There are no words to depict the emotions of the heart that arise when death is called but a "sleep." Lazarus was asleep, and Jesus was going to wake him. What the disciples were about to experience was going to enlarge their trust in God, and one disciple in particular was about to have his faith increased . . . just a little. Thomas reveals his doubtful heart by naively saying that they would go with Jesus so that they could die with Him. I suspect he hadn't heard a word Jesus had just said about knowing what He was doing, and being in total control.

No Big Deal

It was a two day journey, and by the time Jesus and His disciples neared

Bethany, Lazarus had died. Many of the Jews joined Mary and Martha to comfort them concerning the death of the one they so loved.

When Martha heard that Jesus had *finally* arrived, she found Him and immediately let Him know her mind by saying that if He had been there, Lazarus wouldn't have died.

The extra two day wait was a test of the faith of all who professed to love Jesus. Did they trust Him, or did they love the fact that He could do miracles? Is our worship of God conditional upon the fact that God runs to our requests? Does the child love the father because of who the father is, or because he caters to his every desire? The way to reveal the heart, is for the father to wait for a while when a directive comes from the child, and that is what Jesus did in the case of Mary and Martha. Did their hearts become sick as their hope was deferred? Did the acid of bitterness settle in their souls? Was their faith in God greater than anything life could throw in their face? Was their homage conditional?

God's ways are distinctively and consistently different from ours. God did not rescue Daniel out of the lion's den as we would have. He didn't turn off the fiery furnace into which Shadrach, Meshach and Abed-Nego were cast, as we would. He didn't kill Pharaoh and save Moses and His children from the Red Sea, instead He worked His wondrous purposes *in* the lion's den, *in* the furnace, and *in* the Red Sea. Lion's teeth, fire and water are no big deal to the God who created them. Death, at the presence of the Light of the World, is but a shadow that quickly dissipates like a frightened and sickly child.

The two days that Jesus waited, speak to us of the "two days" the Lord has waited in Heaven, rather than coming immediately to this sick and dying world. His two days are as two thousand years to us (2 Peter 3:8), but He is patiently waiting, not willing that any should perish, but that all come to repentance. His purpose is to wait so that the Son might be glorified in us.

Martha's faith in Jesus was unwavering. She said that God would give Him anything He asked. Jesus knew what she was saying beneath that statement, and told her that her brother would rise again. She believed the Scriptures, and knew that the day would come when God would raise the dead, and all humanity would stand before Him in judgment.

Then came a stirring statement. It was a declaration that dwarfed every giant comment from every distinguished human being, like the universe overshadows an atom.

His words were spoken through the lowliness of a human vessel, but they should ring throughout the heavens like the thunder of the greatest storm this world has ever seen.

Jesus said to her,

"I am the resurrection and the life. He who believes in Me, though he may die, he shall live. And whoever lives and believes in Me shall never die."

Jesus asked Martha if she *believed* what He said. Some don't think belief is important, yet our beliefs govern our actions and even our eternal destiny.

There are different categories of belief. For example, we don't need "faith" to know that God exists. We *know,* through the intellect, that a builder exists because of the building. The build*ing* is proof there was a build*er*.

You don't need faith to know there was a builder, all you need is eyes and a working brain. Neither do we need faith to know of God's existence:

"For the invisible things of Him from the creation of the world *are clearly seen (eyes), being understood (working brain) by the things that are made* . . . so they are without excuse" (Romans 1:19, italics added).

If I wanted, however, the builder to *construct* something for me, then I have to have faith in him, and he that comes to God must "believe that He is" (Hebrews 11:6), because if he denies the obvious, then he is in rebellion, and therefore cannot please God. Of course faith is necessary for salvation, but the Creator's existence is axiomatic, because of creation.

If I, however, do deny the obvious and believe that there is no God, I will live my life accordingly. If I believe that all God requires of me, is that I live a good life, and that repentance is not necessary to salvation, I will live my life according to that belief, to my eternal detriment.

But if I believe the testimony of scripture, I will have to radically change my direction. The Bible tells us we will die because we have broken an eternal law— the Law of God. All we need to do is put ourselves on the stand for a moment, face the Law of God, and ask if we have ever told a lie (even a "white" lie)? Have we ever taken something that belonged to another person? If we have been honest and answered "yes," then, by our own admission, we are lying thieves . . . *and we haven't even looked at the other eight Commandments!* God's Law requires "truth in the inward parts;" that means if we "lust," we have committed adultery in our heart, to "hate" is to be a murderer. If we study the Ten Commandments (Exodus 20), we will see that we have all sinned against God, and on Judgment Day we will be found guilty, and condemned to Hell.

I once spoke to a woman who said that there was nothing wrong with lust. To her, there was nothing wrong with *looking*. I asked her if she saw anything wrong with pornography. I said that was just "looking." She saw the point. God's Law includes "intent." If we are given to sexual fantasies, sensual imaginations, then God holds us as guilty as if we had carried out the deed. Some may think such a standard is unfair because the standard is too high, but even civil law carries its justice to that degree. If you are found to be scheming to assassinate the President of the United States, you will come under the wrath of civil law, even though you didn't carry out the deed.

Martha answered Jesus' question about her own beliefs by saying, "Yes, Lord, I believe that You are the Christ, the Son of God, who is come into the world," and from what we know, she lived her life accordingly.

It was then that Martha left Jesus and *secretly* called her sister. "Secretly" perhaps because she knew that Mary was grieved that Jesus had not responded earlier. Her reaction to the fact that Jesus wanted to see her may not have been something Martha wanted others to witness. The devil has easy access when the shield of faith is not held high over the heart, and when death strikes a loved one, doubt can bring with it a fear that God has no concern for our pain.

Yet, a personal word from Jesus can bring peace to a troubled soul. As soon as she heard that the Master was calling for her privately, she quickly went to Him.

Those who were with her, saw her get up and leave, and presumed that she had gone to the tomb to weep. In fact, it seems she didn't say a word to a soul, but went straight to Jesus.

That's what we should do when trouble comes our way—quickly take it to the Lord in prayer. When we walk in repentance and faith, we have a direct hot-line to our Heavenly Father.

Lord, Come and See

When Mary saw Jesus, she fell at His feet, and reiterated the words spoken to Him by Martha: "Lord, if you had been here, my brother would not have died." But Jesus didn't answer her with the same words He gave her sister. He merely inquired where Lazarus lay, and they said, "Lord, come and see."

The Scriptures now give us insight into the spirit of the Son of God. They tell us that when He saw the grieving of Mary and the Jews, He "groaned in the spirit" and was troubled. The Greek word used is *embrimaomai,* and means "to have indignation." He may have been indignant because of their unbelief, because if Bible chronologists have calculated correctly, just over one year earlier He had raised the widow's son in Galilee, and a short time after that raised the daughter of Jairus from the dead. In other portions of scripture, we see where unbelief hindered Jesus from doing "mighty works" (Matthew 13:58), made Jesus "marvel" (Mark 6:6), and brought a rebuke from the Son of God (Mark 16:14). If Mary and Martha had true faith in Him, they would have rejoiced that He would raise

Lazarus, therefore their anguish was evidence that they had limited confidence in His ability.

He also may have been indignant because death had torn this godly family apart. Death is the enemy of humanity, and is said to be the last enemy that shall be destroyed (1 Corinthians 15:26). Indignation should grip the heart of every Christian when he sees death tear apart families. We should be incensed that the god of this world has blinded the minds of those who do not believe. We should be enraged that families grieve without hope, simply because they haven't believed and obeyed the Gospel of Salvation.

Then scripture gives us the smallest, and yet one of the most profound statements in the Bible:

"Jesus wept."

In one sense, this verse is a mystery because Jesus knew what He was about to do. He was about to give Mary and Martha the greatest gift outside of salvation they could ever dare hope for. Yet, He wept.

The prophets tell us that the Messiah would be a "man of sorrows, acquainted with grief" (Isaiah 53:3). He was moved with compassion for the multitudes, wept over Jerusalem, and knew what it was to "weep with those who weep." Even though we have Heaven before us, it pains the Head of the Body when the foot hurts. Jesus is a High Priest who is "touched with the feeling of our infirmities."

When the Jews saw His tears, they saw them as evidence of His love for Lazarus, and it is when we weep with those who weep, that the world will see our love for each other. When one part of the Body of Christ hurts, the whole Body should empathize with it.

Some, in this incident seemed mystified by the tears, perhaps thinking that they were an indication that Jesus could now do nothing in the face of death, asking that if He opened blind eyes, should He not have been able to heal Lazarus?

Grave Consequences

As Jesus approached the tomb, He again groaned within Himself. When He gave instructions for the stone to be rolled away, Martha revealed that she had no idea what Jesus was about to do, by warning Him that the corpse would have already begun the process of decomposition. Jesus gently chided her for her lack of faith, by reminding her that He had said that if she believed, she would see the glory of God.

The reason why Jesus waited for four days may have been because Jewish tradition said that the soul stayed around the body for three days, but on the fourth day it left the body permanently. On the fourth day, even to the traditional Jew, Lazarus was therefore, door-nail dead.

After the stone was removed from the tomb, Jesus lifted His eyes up to Heaven and said, "I thank You that You have heard Me," directly followed by, "And I know that You always hear Me, but because of the people who are standing by I said this, that they may believe that You sent Me." He had implicit, absolute and perfect faith in God. There had never been one sin to make a separation between Him and His Father. So, because the words, "I thank You that You have heard Me" contained an insinuation that there was a possibility that God would not hear Him, He immediately followed it with, "I know that You always hear Me," and then He gave the reason why He said those words. They were said, not for His sake, but for ours.

There is another reason that the Father always heard the prayers of the Son. The

Apostle Paul says of Jesus, "He was heard in that He feared" (Hebrews 5:7). Jesus had due reverence for God. I shudder when I hear professing Christians say things like, "*I got mad at God!*" Such statements reveal a lack of the most necessary of virtues, the fear of the Lord, which is the beginning of wisdom.

The thought that Jesus would get angry at the Father is offensive. The child of God who walks in the fear of the Lord will say, "My flesh trembles for fear of You" (Psalm 119:120), "Though He slay me, yet will I praise Him." He would rather die than hold his angry fist up at God.

When Jesus said these things, He cried with a loud voice for Lazarus to come out of the tomb. *All Hell held its defiled breath.* Up until the incarnation, it was the *devil* who had the power of death (Hebrews 2:14), and now his dominion was being challenged by the offspring of Adam. This single Seed was about to bruise his horny head (Genesis 3:15).

The words of Jesus cut through the icy grip of death like a white-hot blade through soft powdered snow. The same Word that brought life in the beginning, breathed life into the decomposing corpse of Lazarus. Suddenly, from the blackened shadow of the tomb appeared a figure, wrapped in grave clothes. As he stood at the entrance of the tomb (for tombs didn't need an *exit* until that day), his face and body were covered with grave clothes. God took him by the hand and led him to the light.

What a picture of that which is before us! The hour is coming when *all* that are in their graves will hear His voice. The victory Lazarus had over death was bad news for the devil and the undertaker, but it was only a temporary triumph, for the undertaker would eventually get his deathly fee. Lazarus would ultimately depart from this earth, but the time is coming when death shall be no more. On that day, we will exchange these vile, perishing bodies for incorruptible bodies that will never feel pain, disease, or taste the bitterness of death:

> "So when this corruptible has put on incorruption, and this mortal has put on immortality, then shall be brought to pass the saying that is written: `Death is swallowed up in victory'" (1 Corinthians 15:54)

For those who trust in Jesus, this body is but a chrysalis, which may become wrinkled and crusty with age, but it is just a shell that will be dropped off as the new butterfly emerges.

Who could not fall on his face after witnessing such a scene and cry, *"God is with us!"* Who could not rejoice with unspeakable joy at seeing death vanquished with one word from Jesus of Nazareth?

Rhetoric though it may seem, there is a sad answer. Although many of the Jews who witnessed the raising of Lazarus believed, *some didn't.* They rushed to the chief priests and reported the happenings at the tomb.

The panicked Pharisees must have had shares in the undertaking business. They hurriedly gathered together a council meeting, and in a frenzy asked what they could do. The whole world was going after Him, but instead of acknowledging that this was indeed the Messiah, they were worried about their own ambitions. The Romans had conquered the Jewish nation, but for the sake of harmony in Israel, they set up four governing authorities in the nation. If the Jewish authorities relinquished certain rights, such as capital punishment among other things, they were given a religious autonomy. If they exceeded their religious bounds by establishing a king, there was a real threat that the Romans would come and crush them.

Despite the shadowy nature of where their conversation was heading, God sent light right into their midst. Caiaphas, the high priest unwittingly prophesied that Jesus would die for the sins of the nation of Israel, and for the sins of the world.

Learning From the Pupil

In 1993, a 4-year-old girl became sick with what her parent's thought was merely a virus. As time passed, she became so ill, they rushed her to the nearby hospital. By the time she arrived, she was clinically dead, so doctors and staff immediately began emergency procedures on her now ceased heart. After 20 minutes a special emergency team of ten people were called in and began a procedure where they put so much pressure with CPR on the child's flexible rib cage, it would have crushed that of an adult. After an incredible 41 minutes, the little girl's heart began beating again, making this the longest time in known history that someone survived heart cessation, without brain damage. The reason the doctors did not give up when others thought the child was dead, was simply because they could see that the child's pupil's were still responding to light, which meant that the brain was not yet dead.

The Pharisees, however, were brain dead. The refused to receive the light which came by the Law, and each time God gave them light, their pupils remained lifeless.

Like the emergency team, the Ten Commandments were given to put pressure on our hearts (Romans 3:19), in the hope that we may respond to the light of the glorious Gospel (Galatians 3:24), yet tragically many, like the stubborn Pharisees, remain in the cold grip of being dead in trespasses and sins.

From that day on, their murderous hearts were knit together. They would put this Jesus of Nazareth to death if it was the last thing they would do. No longer would His words stir them to just a reactionary killing, they would premeditate and conspire to cut Him off from the land of the living.

One of our neighbors once came over to see us with her pet parrot on her shoulder. It was an attractive (and expensive) bird with brightly colored yellow wings, a green head, and a large beak. As she spoke to us, it said a friendly, *"Hi, how are ya?"* It was obviously concerned about my well-being. I smiled and couldn't resist reaching out my finger to stroke it, when suddenly the evil beast bit into the nail of my finger with a vice-grip. I screamed and instinctively pulled my hand down at such a speed, the bird (still holding onto my finger) bounced off the ground.

The Pharisees were like our neighbor's bird. Their outward appearance was attractive, but they merely parroted their dead religion. They drew near to God with their lips, but their insincere hearts were far from Him. Their many questions directed at Jesus didn't come from a desire to know the truth; all they wanted was an opportunity to attack Him with the sharp beak of the enmity they had for God.

Therefore, Jesus no longer walked openly among the Jews, but remained in the wilderness of Ephraim with His disciples. When the time of the Passover came, and many went to Jerusalem for the purification rights, the Jews wondered if He would go there. If He did, the chief priests and the Pharisees had given a command that they should report it, that they might seize Him.

Jesus was a wanted Man.

Chapter Twelve
Dollar Signs in the Eyes

The life of Jesus of Nazareth is focused on the passover that came in what is commonly called "the year of His popularity," the third year of His ministry. This passover was when the Lamb of God would be sacrificed for the sins of the world. This was the "hour" for which He was born. To understand the wondrous and yet solemn moment in history, we must go back to Israel at the time of Moses.

God promised to deliver His people from the iron furnace of Egypt, and to do so, He raised Moses as a deliverer. Mighty signs and wonders were given to Egypt; then, as a culmination of the plagues, the angel of death was to pass through the land. Israel was told:

"But against none of the children of Israel shall a dog move its tongue, against man or beast, that you may know that the Lord does make a difference between the Egyptians and Israel" (Exodus 11:7).

They were then told to:

1. Take a lamb.

2. Make sure the lamb was without blemish.

3. Kill it at twilight.

4. Apply the blood to the doorposts.

5. Eat it with bitter herbs.

6. Eat all of it.

7. Be fully clothed and ready to go.

8. Have knowledge of the coming judgment.

9. Remove leaven from their house.

10. Remember to rest.

As we saw at the beginning of the Gospel of John, Jesus was the Lamb provided by God (John 1:29).

He was sinless, without blemish (1 Peter 1:9).

As we will see in the following chapters, He suffered on the cross and tasted death for every man, and when He did so, a twilight darkness fell upon the whole land (Matthew 27:45).

Now, all who apply the blood of the Lamb of God to the doorposts of their lives, have the angel of death pass over them (2 Timothy 1:10).

Contrary to the teaching of modern thought, there is a bitterness that accompanies genuine conversion. When repentance grips a sinner, his laughter is "turned to mourning" and his "joy to heaviness." The contrite soul experiences the fear of God, the fear of the Law, and the fear of eternal punishment, as he understands that the wrath of God abides on him. His sins go over his head and weigh heavy upon him, causing him to labor and be heavy laden. He experiences a godly sorrow which works repentance (2 Corinthians 7:10-11).

When he partakes of the Lamb of God, he does so with total commitment (1 Corinthians 11:29).

The Christian is then to be fully "clothed with humility" (1 Peter 5:5).

He is always ready to take the Gospel to every creature (Mark 16:16).

The leaven of false doctrine must be purged from the life of the believer, and the reason cited by scripture is that "Christ our passover was sacrificed for us" (1 Corinthians 5:7).

As the Christian trusts in the finished work of Calvary's cross, he enters into the "rest" of God, "for we who have believed do enter that rest" (Hebrews 4:3).

Offended by Worship

It was six days before the passover when Jesus spent some time with His friends at Bethany. As Martha served, the once dead Lazarus was one of those who sat at the table with Jesus. Mary, no doubt with the fresh image of the unthinkable, the raising of her brother from the dead, still on her mind, took some very expensive ointment and anointed the feet of Jesus and wiped them with her hair.

It is hard for those whose understanding is darkened, to understand worship. There is something so deep, so rich, so wonderful about worshipping God, it evades the human mind. There is no earthly analogy, no parallel to which we may compare our Creator. Words of appreciation, adoration, respect and devotion fall infinitely short of the emotions aroused by the revelation of who Jesus of Nazareth is. Mary couldn't put her gratitude into words, so she put it into worship.

As she poured the ointment onto His feet, she was pouring out her very soul at His feet. Then she wiped His feet with her hair. A woman's hair is her "glory" (1 Corinthians 11:15), and in this act of worship, she was laying her glory, the depth of her femininity, at His feet.

This offended one of the disciples. Judas was upset at what he saw. The dollar signs in his eyes hindered him from seeing Jesus clearly. His objection to the "extravagant" nature of what he had seen was rebuked by Jesus, because Jesus saw the reason behind his words. He didn't care for the poor, but was a thief with his fingers in the collection bag he had been trusted with.

Worship of God is offensive to the devil and his proud children. The act is a soul making "her boast in the Lord," and only "the humble will hear and be glad."

But of all who worship God from a pure heart, those who do so with the greatest of commitment should be those who have lived this side of the cross. Mary's deep and beautiful behavior came *before* she had seen the love of Christ manifest in the cross. She knew His kind words, the gentle touch of His loving hand, but she hadn't yet seen the depth of His love so evidently portrayed at Golgotha. That made her sacrifice even more meaningful.

Super Natural Enquirer

Lazarus became a celebrity. He hit the headlines of the tabloids. This was something more than "Wife's Varicose Veins Form Map Leading to Hidden Treasure." Crowds came just to look at this man who *undeniably* came back from the dead, and many went away believing.

It was because of this the homicidal chief priests plotted how they might kill him. Scripture doesn't tell us if Lazarus gave verbal testimony to his experience, but it would be hard to imagine that he didn't. More than likely he was coerced by both friend and stranger to tell what it was like to die, then to come back to life. Such bold testimony will always stir up opposition from man and devil.

The testimony of Lazarus made Jesus even more popular. Great multitudes came to the Passover Feast, then took branches of palm trees and cried out "Hosanna, Blessed is He who comes in the Name of the Lord. The King of Israel!"

This was in accordance with the Law

as a way to express joy (Leviticus 23:40).

Then Jesus did a very unusual thing. Instead of riding triumphantly through the streets of Jerusalem on a kingly white stallion, He chose to ride on a lowly beast of burden, a young donkey. Imagine how humbling it would be for the President of the United States to ride through New York on the back of a donkey. But this is what the King of Kings did, because He wasn't coming in flaming fire, on a white horse with ten thousands of His saints. This time He was coming in lowliness, humbling Himself and becoming obedient to the death of the cross.

Not only was the life of Lazarus a witness to the power of Jesus of Nazareth over death, but "the people, who were with Him when He called Lazarus out of the tomb and raised him from the dead, bore witness." This brought even more people to meet Jesus, causing the Pharisees to throw up their hands in frustration and say, "You see that you are accomplishing nothing. Look, the world has gone after Him!" *Would to God that were true nowadays.*

Sir, We Would See Jesus

Certain Greeks from Bethsaida came to the feast, found Philip and said to him,

"Sir, we would see Jesus." The disciples told Jesus, but Jesus didn't say, "Show them in." Instead, He spoke of the cross—His hour. He said how a grain of wheat must fall to the ground and die before it can produce more grain.

He then used both paradox and hyperbole, saying that if a person loves his life, he will lose it, and he who *hates* it will keep it for eternity. The true servant of Christ will follow Him wherever He goes, and will have the inconceivable honor of being honored by God.

It is a sad testimony to humanity that, like a mad dog, it bites the Hand that feeds it. God gave us our very existence. He tells us how we can live forever, simply by yielding our lives into His care. Those who refuse to, will eventually forfeit the very thing they are trying to preserve.

The Greeks from Bethsaida wanted to see the Jesus who did miracles, the popular King of Israel, but there was another viewpoint of Jesus they must see. These men, by the humble spirit in which they asked to see Jesus, were to be pointed to the cross of Calvary. The viewpoint they had to behold, was to be from the base of a bloody cross.

The Coming Suffering

Just speaking of the hour He was to soon face, sent Jesus into prayer. But what could He ask of the Father? There was little consolation, because for this hour He came to this earth

When He prayed, "Father, glorify Your name," a thunderous voice from Heaven answered that He had both glorified it and will glorify it again.

Perhaps this is a reference to when God glorified His Name through Moses, and would also do it through this Prophet who was raised up like Moses.

The cross was a demonstration of the righteousness of God revealed from Heaven. It was God's judgment upon the sin of the world as it was laid upon the Savior, and when that was done, it stripped from the accuser of the brethren, his power to accuse, and his power over death.

When Jesus was lifted up on the cross, as He had years earlier told Nicodemus, He would draw all men to Himself. When the crowd was mystified as to what He meant, He gave them almost identical words He gave to His disciples before He raised Lazarus, saying that they should walk in the light while the light was with them. He also told them that darkness would "overtake" them if they didn't remain in the light. How true that is. If we don't walk from sin, sin will overtake us. The darkness of iniquity is not passive. It is an aggressive enemy seeking to devour us; an enemy we must continually contest for territory.

Those who trust in Jesus were called the children of light, reminding us of the words of Paul the Apostle:

"The night is far spent, the day is at hand. Therefore let us cast off the works of darkness, and let us put on the armor of light" (Romans 13:12).

After He said these things, He departed and was hidden from them.

Despite all the miracles that issued from His hands, the majority of the Jews failed to believe that He was the promised Messiah, fulfilling the words of Isaiah the prophet (Isaiah 6:9-10). Many of the rulers however, did believe, but they were fearful of being put out of the synagogue and would not confess Him publicly. They didn't want to lose their seat in the synagogue.

Their problem was the fact that they loved the approval of men, more than the approval of God.

Then Jesus reiterated what He had been saying all along:

1. He who believes in Jesus, believes in God.

2. He who sees Jesus, sees God.

3. He was come as a light in the world.

4. Whoever believes in Him would not abide in darkness.

5. He who rejects His words would be judged by them.

6. He did not come to judge, but that the world might be saved through Him.

7. He did not speak on His own authority.

8. God gave Him the words which He spoke.

9. God's command was everlasting life.

10. He was only obeying the Father when He spoke.

Chapter Thirteen
The Devil Made Me Do It

It was just before the feast of the passover, and Jesus knew that His hour had come. He was about to be torn from His beloved disciples. The Scriptures tell us that He loved His own until the *end*. He loved them to the uttermost, and was about to bring His devotion to the pinnacle of the cross.

After supper, the devil put betrayal into the heart of Judas Iscariot. While *"the devil made me do it,"* will not be a valid defence on Judgment Day, if more would believe that the hand of the devil is at work in their lives, our prisons would be less full, and human suffering would be much less.

So often we hear of people feeling

"compelled" to kill, and thinking the impulses were their own. If potential homosexuals understood the influence of unclean spirits, they would be less likely to follow every grimy impulse that comes into their minds. Those who believe that our battle is not against flesh and blood, but demonic personalities, will then be less prone to be tools of darkness.

The godly will acknowledge that they were once part of those in whom the spirit of disobedience works. If a thought violates the conscience (whether it be from their own heart or from Hell), they resist it steadfast in the faith. They guard their hearts with all diligence, because out of it proceeds the issues of life.

In Thailand, there is a national treasure made of solid gold, worth millions of dollars, but as the public file passed it, there is a strange absence of armed guards. In fact, there are *no* guards. This is because the building that houses it has been built with doors too small to remove the priceless treasure.

The godly guards his heart will all diligence, not with the armed guards of legalism, but by building his house with the lowly doors of humility, faith, and obedience to the Spirit of God. A sinful thought may get in, but it will be turned back, and leave without taking any of the "treasure in earthen vessels."

However, the *unbelieving* heart concludes that the sinful thought that enters his mind is merely his own. If a homosexual thought invades his heart, and comes fast and often, the ignorant sinner concludes that is his born desire. The door is then cracked open to the devil, and he takes possession of the house. The ungodly man who finds a strong and persistent thought of adultery in his heart, rather than resist it steadfast in the faith as do the godly, cultivates it and lets the poisonous tree take root, destroying an otherwise happy marriage.

Jesus warned,

"Out of the heart proceed evil thoughts, murders, adulteries, fornications, thefts, false witness, blasphemies" (Matthew 15:19).

The human heart is the devil's playground. The unfenced playground of Judas Iscariot's covetous heart led him into theft. It is a great leap from theft to betrayal, but perhaps the devil was able to make that jump by giving him thoughts of betrayal, because he first cracked open the door through a jealousy of Jesus. Jealousy may have unlocked the entrance to hatred, and hatred welcomed betrayal and murder and its fearful consequences, with open arms.

What Judas did was inexcusable. Two thousand years after his betrayal, his name still carries with it connotations of evil (do you know any parents who have called their children "Judas?").

Names are interesting things. Not many people know what Adam's last name was. Think about it. What was the last name of Adam and Eve? The answer is in the genealogies listed in Luke chapter 3. In that list you find that Nathan was the "son of David." Nowadays we would more than likely call him *Nathan Davidson*. If he was the son of John, we would call him *Nathan Johnson*, or the son of Peter, he would be called *Nathan Peterson*, etc.

At the top of the list in Luke (3:38), it says, " . . . the son of Seth, the son of Adam, the son of God." Adam was the original "son of God." So the name of the mailbox outside the Garden of Eden would have been "Adam and Eve Godson."

Scripture speaks of Judas Iscariot when it says, "Let his days be few, and let another take his office (see Acts 1:20) . . . let his posterity be cut off, and in the generation following let their name be blotted out" (Psalm 109: 8,13). For years, I have visited different cities, and have checked telephone books to see if there are any "Iscariots," and I haven't yet found any. His name has been "blotted out" (if I do find one, I may give them a call and tell them to change their name, quickly).

Humility Indeed

Jesus then rose from supper, laid aside His garments, took a towel, girded Himself and began to humbly wash His disciple's feet. After He had done so, He took His garments again, sat down and asked them if they knew what He had done for them.

Here is wonderful typology—Jesus rose from His throne in Heaven, left His communion with the Father, laid aside His garments of light, girded Himself with human flesh, and then poured out his soul to death in the ultimate service of humanity. He "humbled Himself and became obedient to death, even the death of the cross."

After He had done this deed, He again took His garments, sat down at the right hand of God, and now says to us, "Do you know what I have done for you?"

Here, at the feet of the disciples, is the ultimate in humility. The Creator of the universe, not only humbled Himself to become a man, but He condescended to wash the feet of sinful man. One can't help but identify with Peter. He was aghast at the thought that Jesus would do such a lowly servant's duty, but here is He who is meek and lowly of heart, showing us how we should treat one another.

Jesus washed the feet of humanity, but hidden within this feat of humility is the thought that even though we are washed upon conversion, we need to continually wash our feet of the daily dirt we pick up as we walk through this sinful world.

We should never let a day go by without a search of the soul for those sins that so easily beset us. Wrong attitudes, hidden motives, holier-than-thou condescension, lack of love for the lost, and other secret and subtle sins, like unseen dust, can softly fall on us and after time, cling to our flesh as a foul grime.

Although we are told to humble ourselves, life itself often does that for us. I heard of a well-known preacher who took his jacket off while preaching and had the humbling incident of finding that a sock had stuck to his shirt through static. It must have been caught in the sleeve of the jacket. Let's hope he had something else up his sleeve   spiritually.

The following words sum up how we should think of ourselves:

Sometime when you're feeling important;
Sometime when your ego's in bloom;
Sometime when you take it for granted,
You're the best qualified in the room.

Sometime when you feel that your going
Would leave an unfillable hole,
Just follow this simple instruction
And see how it humbles your soul.

Take a bucket and fill it with water,
Put your hand in it up to the wrist;
Pull it out and the hole that's remaining
Is the measure of how you'll be missed.

Splash all you please when you enter,
You can stir up the water galore;
But stop and you'll find in a minute
That it looks quite the same as before.

The moral in this quaint example
Is to do just the best you can.
Be proud of yourself, but remember
There's no indispensable man.

For some reason, the author didn't sign the poem. Perhaps he realized how good it was.

Speaking of humility, and the gift of circumstantial humblings—I was once picked up from Dallas airport in a black limousine, and taken to a large Bible school where I was to speak for a week. As I sat in the spacious vehicle, I called Sue on the car phone and said, "Guess where I'm calling from?" and spent some time crowing about the limo.

As we drove through the streets of Dallas, I did the presidential wave to the crowds, but they didn't seem to wave back. When we arrived at my room, I got out of the car and realized why the crowds hadn't lined the streets. The windows of the limo were tinted and they couldn't see who I was!

I went into my room, made myself a bowl of cornflakes, and with them in hand (still on cloud nine) I called Sue to brag again about the limo ride. As I dialed, I bumped the bowl of cornflakes and they spilled into the top pocket of my shirt. There is something so unpresidential about strained milk pouring out of the bottom of one's shirt pocket. There is also something sobering, down-to-earth and humbling about the experience of reaching into one's shirt pocket and pulling out handfuls of cold, wet cornflakes.

Improving Your Serve

All the disciples but one were washed. We can only wonder what went through the mind of both Jesus and Judas, as his feet were being washed by his so-called Lord and Master.

The servant who considers himself to be greater than his master will not serve him from the heart. Believers are servants of the Most High God, and servants to a most lowly world. The moment we forget that we ourselves were once "serving different lusts and pleasures, living in malice and envy, hateful and hating one another," we will forget that we are their servants. The proud spirit of condescension will see the world as sinners rather than potential saints. But those whose greatest joy and supreme aim is to do the will of God, will be good and faithful servants, presenting the Gospel to an undeserving world on the golden plate of humility.

Jesus then told the disciples to imitate Him. The world is full of imitators. Did you know that in an unofficial count, there were 216 "Elvis impersonators" in the United States in 1960? By 1970 there were 2,400. By 1980, there were an estimated 6,300; in 1992 there were 14,000, which means by the year 2010, one in four people in the U.S. will be an Elvis impersonator. Thrilling prospect.

Death Grip

It was immediately after Jesus washed the feet of Judas, that He became troubled in spirit and warned that one of them would betray Him. *But who could it be?* As far as the disciples were concerned, He was surrounded by loyal and loving friends. He so trusted one, He allowed him to be in charge of the finances that came to the ministry. These were those who ate bread with Him—His "family," and He was saying that one would try and betray Him? Such was the cloak of deceit, that not one of the disciples suspected Judas Iscariot.

Peter asked John to ask Jesus who this was who could do such a thing, so Jesus told them that it was he who dipped bread with Him. After Judas dipped bread in the dish with the Savior, satan himself took total possession of him. He mortgaged his home to the devil.

The word "mort-gage" means "death grip," and it was that to which Judas opened himself.

Even when he went out into the darkness to betray Jesus, some of the disciples didn't suspect him, but rather thought that he had gone to give money to the poor.

Judasless Intimacy

After the leaving of Judas, Jesus opens a deep, rich communion with His disciples. The day will also come when all the betrayers, who profess to be disciples will go out into the outer darkness of eternity. They will also be with the devil they so willingly served. Those left in the Kingdom of God, when the goats are separated from the sheep, will have intimate communion with Him in whose presence is fullness of joy, and at whose right hand is pleasure forevermore.

Then begins some most peculiar words from Jesus. He is about to begin the hour of His suffering, yet He says, "Now the Son of man is glorified, and God is glorified in Him. If God is glorified in Him, God will also glorify Him in Himself, and glorify Him immediately." It was the leaving of Judas which seemed to spark the talk of His glory. Perhaps it was a reference to the fact that, despite the shadow which was about to cover Him, the sunshine of God's glory would still shine above the dark clouds of Calvary.

When the one who was a "devil" left, Jesus called his disciples His little children, and warned them again that they were about to be split apart with the axe of the wrath of man, telling them that their love for one another would be a sure sign to the world that they belonged to Him.

When Jesus spoke of being separated from them and going to a place the disciples could not follow, Peter questioned the certainty of what Jesus said, saying that he would lay his life down for Him, but time would show Peter that watery words run places that solid deeds find hard to follow.

Chapter Fourteen
Heart Trouble

The human heart is prone to trouble. The Scriptures tell us that man is *born* to trouble, as sparks fly upwards (Job 5:7). But Jesus told those that trust him, not to *let* their hearts be troubled. The heart of man wants to rule over him. His reason, logic, sense, the wisdom which is "from below," fights faith in God. It will give a thousand reasons why we should be troubled in a lion's den, in a fiery furnace, or at the edge of the Red Sea—but trust refuses the fear that reason and logic bring.

Jesus said, "You believe in God, believe also in Me." Almost everyone believes in God the Creator, but salvation comes only through trusting the Savior. Those who have faith in God *and* Jesus will not let their heart be troubled. They will not fret about evil doers, or about tomorrow's dollar, because tomorrow is in the hands of God.

Faith in God clears the muddy waters of fear. The Christian's confidence in Jesus Christ knows that his eternal footsteps have been ordered by the Lord, that there is a mansion prepared for him that his wildest imaginations could not conceive. If these things weren't so, Jesus would have told us. *He is not a liar.* His word is sure and steadfast, a mooring for the soul, and those who come into the harbor of a calm faith in God have perfect peace in the troubled storms of this world.

What do You Think Paul?

I have often wanted to go back in time, pick up the Apostle Paul from the cold dungeon of the Philippian jail, and sit him in front of my computer. I would take great delight in watching his eyes widen as he sees how a word processor can open sentences and drop thoughts in the middle; how it can "spell" and "grammar" check a document. Then I would show him how a video camera operates, and the miracle of television. I would enjoy seeing him try and figure out how a remote control changes the channel.

I would sit him in my car, drive him through the incredible L.A. freeway system, and show him the huge glass buildings that adorn our city. Then I would take him to the airport, where doors open automatically, and watch his face as he sits in a 747 jumbo, and blasts into the heavens. How could he not be impressed with the miracles of advancement of modern technology, of the incredible progress of mankind! *Easily.* Paul had been to the "third Heaven," where no doubt God's "high tech" makes man's highest pinnacle of high tech seem like the demented scribblings of a dribbling imbecile with a blunt pencil in a dark night of the middle-ages.

How limited we are when we try and imagine Heaven. All we can think of is gold streets and brilliant light. That's about it. But I'm sure if we were more heavenly-minded, we would be more earthly use. If we could just grip some of the glories that shall be ours, we would lay up our treasures in Heaven, looking not at the things that are seen, but at the things that are unseen.

One thing which can help us grasp what the future holds is to realize that God's Kingdom is coming to earth, when His will will be done on earth as it is in Heaven. We won't be, as the world so often depicts, sitting on clouds, playing (rusty) harps. We will rule and reign on this earth, because the New Jerusalem will come down from Heaven to this earth (Revelation 21:2). That's when the curse will be lifted, and lions, wolves and other animals will stop devouring each other. There will be no more wars, famines, floods, earthquakes, disease, suffering and death.

There will, however, be long lines of undertakers at the Millennial Unemployment Department (MUD).

Thomas didn't doubt what Jesus said, but he did ask a question which brought us one of the most profound verses in scripture. When he asked the directions to his mansion, Jesus didn't merely give him the key, he gave him the Door. He gave to him a one sentence answer which annihilated every other religion ever made by man as a means of salvation. He said,

> "I am the way, the truth and the life. No one comes to the Father except through Me."

As a teenager, I remember falling off my surfboard and being pulled "over the falls" by a very powerful wave. For what seemed an eternity, I was tossed like a cork in turbulence beneath the surface of the water. Finally, I was able to take control, and with my lungs nearly bursting, I headed for the surface knowing that at any second I would burst through into fresh air. Suddenly, I felt a clunk! I had gone in the wrong direction and hit the bottom. In panic, I turned around and headed upwards. I still remember the word I said as I burst through the surface. It was a loud and long, *"Pffufffttt!"*

I was *very* sincere in my belief that I was heading towards the surface, but I was going in the wrong direction. The way I should have been heading was up, and I was going down, sincere though I was.

There is only one way to God, and that's through Jesus Christ. All the other religions are no doubt sincere in their beliefs that they are heading in the right direction, but they are the efforts of men, who through their own deeds are seeking the forgiveness of sins. They attempt to induce God to forgive their transgressions by fasting, prayers, lying on beds of nails and all sorts of rituals, but the Messiah was *God's* provision for our sin. Man struggles to get himself out of the quicksand of his sin, but every move only makes him sink deeper. Jesus Christ was the Father's hand reaching down to pull us out.

There is salvation in no other name. There is only one mediator between man and God, the Man Christ Jesus. All that came before Him and all that come after Him, claiming to be the way to God, are thieves and robbers.

When Jesus again spoke of being representative of the Father, Philip asked to see God. More goose-bump material. When Jesus spoke of being an envoy of Heaven, this wasn't the King sending a servant, it was the King Himself. This was God Almighty, the God of Abraham, the God of Creation, disclosed in mortal form. God became man in Christ. He is the express image of the invisible God (Colossians 1:15); "God was manifest in the flesh" (1 Timothy 3:16). If your Bible doesn't say *God* was manifest in the flesh, then get another version.

A Christian is someone to whom the Father has revealed that Jesus is the Christ, the Son of the Living God. His conversion is a work of the Spirit. The world is full of people who profess to know God, and the test as to whether or not they do, is to ask them if Jesus Christ came in the flesh (1 John 4:3, 2 John 1:7). Often they merely have a head knowledge, rather than a heart experience.

I once spoke to a man in his early 40's

who said he had read the Bible from cover to cover, four or five times while in prison. He was into fornication, said that his god "was his brain," and believed in what he mistakenly called, "Darwin's Theory of *Revolution.*" His words revealed the smallness of his brain-god.

The day Philip asked Jesus to reveal the Father, he realized that he hadn't seen the forest for the trees. What is God like?—look to Jesus, both in His incarnate state, and as the glorified Christ. The Bible says of Him that the sun shines in His strength, and that He is coming in "flaming fire to take vengeance on those who know not God and obey not the Gospel of our Lord Jesus Christ." The words of Jesus were words of the Father. God was in Christ, bringing the world to Himself.

One Tough Cookie

The unlearned look at the promises of Christ and fail to realize that these are for "disciples," and those *disciplined* to Him will only desire that which is in accordance with His will. They ask, no longer motivated by greed, but that the Father may be glorified in the Son. They love Him, therefore they keep His commandments. They have yielded their sinful hearts to Him and been made new creatures in Christ. They have loved Him and have been loved of the Father, and therefore have the manifestation of Christ in them, the Hope of Glory.

A young pastor once went to a Chinese restaurant and purchased a "fortune cookie," removed the fortune note with a pair of tweezers and slipped in his own typed note, which said, "You are about to be proposed to by the man of your dreams." He then asked the staff to serve that cookie after a dinner he was about to have with his girlfriend.

After the meal, as they opened their cookies he said, "What does yours say?" She said, "You wouldn't believe it!" and wouldn't tell him until he coaxed it out of her; then he presented the engagement ring. The following Sunday, he stood up in his church and said how he had met so many wonderful people since he came to live in the area. He named a few, then referred to his girlfriend, turned to her father, who was sitting with his wife in church and said, "By the way Mr. So n'so, I would be honored if you would give me permission to take your daughter's hand in marriage." The place erupted.

All who partake in salvation become part of a wonderful and divine romance.

We are the "espoused virgin," betrothed to the Prince of Peace. As Jesus sat at the last supper with His disciples, He presented His love to them, but this would be demonstrated—the cross of Calvary was given to humanity as an expression of His fathomless love. In the Divine romance, the Father's permission wasn't left until after the presentation of the ring; the Father was in the Son, uniting the world to Himself.

Buffalo and Geese

During this intimate time, Jesus spoke of the promise of the Father. He would give them the "earnest of the Spirit."

Back in the 1980's, the owner of a small company took an objective look at his business and realized that his employees were like a herd of buffalo. Buffalo need leadership. If there is no leader, they stand around and do nothing. That's why the early settlers were able to slaughter so many so quickly. This businessman watched his workers work with minimal commitment to the cause. They did what they were told until it was time to go home.

The reason for this became clear to him. He was the only one who had a real interest in his company, so he spent some time studying the way geese fly, and found that they change leadership regularly, and land as a group. So, he radically changed his business by spreading the leadership role, giving each of his employees a share in the profits. The result was that the company prospered incredibly.

In giving His Holy Spirit, God has given the believer great interest in the Kingdom of God. He allows places of leadership. He is no longer a Leader who stands afar off, but He lives within the believer to will and do of His good pleasure. It is His good pleasure to give us the Kingdom. He has great rewards for those that love Him, and He gives us "righteousness, peace and joy in the Holy Spirit" until the full payment comes.

His peace is not the peace which the world gives. The world's peace is merely absence of war or noise, but the peace of God passes all understanding, and keeps our hearts and minds in Christ Jesus. It is a peace that remains in the lion's den, in the storm, at the Red Sea, because it is not a peace which depends on circumstances, but upon the knowledge that God has all things in dominion.

Also within this passage is adequate material for the unlearned to take scripture out of context and build a church upon it. "My Father is greater than I," is a foundation for the false teachings of the so-called *"Jehovah's* Witnesses," who suppose that Jesus was conceding that Jehovah was God and He was a lesser, created deity. However, other verses give light on the subject. When Jehovah became a Man in Jesus of Nazareth, He limited Himself to a human body, and while He was in Christ, obviously the Father was greater. He was not only made lower than God, He was made lower than the angels—"But we see Jesus, who was made a little lower than the angels for the suffering of death" (Hebrews 2:9).

I Will Not Leave You Comfortless

Jesus told His disciples that the Holy Spirit would come and bring things to their (and our) remembrance. I am so thankful for His help. As life passes by, so does the ability to learn and remember things. Each week I teach a Bible study, through an interpreter, to about 80 Mexicans. It took me about six months just to learn how to say "God bless you" in Spanish. I would learn it, say it one week, then have to look up the wording the following week to refresh my memory. I had seen Mexicans tell their dogs to "sit, lie down, roll over and fetch," in Spanish, and the dogs would obey. That made me feel stupid—that a dog could speak Spanish, when I couldn't even remember a few words!

Jesus said that when the Holy Spirit came, He would dwell *within* the believer. Here is more evidence that Jesus Christ is God. He said, "I will not leave you comfortless, I will come unto you." The Apostle Paul called the Holy Spirit, the "Spirit of Christ" (Romans 8:9), while Peter tells us that the Prophets of the Old Testament had the "Spirit of Christ" in them (1 Peter 1:11). Jesus Christ is God the Holy Spirit, and through the power of His Spirit, He never leaves nor forsakes those who trust in Him.

The world sings songs in which they promise to never leave nor forsake the one they love, but the cold hard truth is that death will rip each of us from our loved ones. We will pass through death alone, unless we have our hand in the hand of Jesus.

I was once present when an elderly lady left this life and went into the next. She loved the Lord, and her godly children sat around her, holding her hand and singing, "Turn your eyes upon Jesus."

How different from the terror of passing into the blackness of death without faith in Jesus Christ.

God often confirms His presence with the Christian. The skeptic may call these incidents "co-incidents," but God's children know better. They also know that their confidence in God is not based on things that happen to confirm His presence, but on the immutability of His promise —that it's impossible for Him to lie. He is always with us, even if the confirmations are few and far between, or even if they are non-existent.

In April of 1994, I was ministering in a small church in Iowa. I had traveled a great distance, both by plane and car to get there, and God encouraged me at the end of the last service in which I spoke. The music leader chose a song which, for some reason, brought tears to my eyes. As I listened, it sounded very much like a Maori tune. Maoris are the native people of New Zealand, my home country. But this song was a hymn with *Christian* words. I looked up the first line on the chorus in the index of the hymn book, and found the words "Maori melody" at the top of the hymn.

I was so heartened to think that God would condescend to move the song leader to choose a hymn (out of a hymnal of over 500 hymns) to encourage me. The song leader had no idea that the song was of New Zealand origin. That small incident reminded me of the fact that God was intimately familiar with my every move, my every thought, and every heart's desire. Still, it may have been a coincidence.

The following weekend, I flew to Dallas, Texas. After three nights of ministry, I finished my last sermon, and sat down on the chair on the platform, when I suddenly felt overcome with emotion. I stopped what I was doing and listened to the hymn being played by the choir director. I hadn't told anyone at that church about the Maori hymn, but that was what he was playing on the piano.

Chapter Fifteen
A Lesson in Gardening

It was appropriate for Jesus to talk to his disciples about pruning, because those who made up this small vine were about to be pruned radically. The sharp and biting shears of persecution were about to divide the disciples, and those without the knowledge that God uses and even *brings* about troublesome times, would be thrown into confusion and fear. Again, Jesus emphasized the fact that love is proven by obedience, pointing to the cross, in which He would prove His love by laying down His life.

The World's Hatred

The comforting words Jesus gave to His disciples were fitting because they were about to be witnesses of a spearhead of hatred for their beloved Teacher. They had attested the adoring praise of those who lined the streets of Jerusalem, and now they were going to witness the mocking condemnation of those who hate God without cause.

I received a letter once from a Christian who witnessed to a friend on many different occasions, but when he began using God's Law, his friend got up from the table and stormed off. He had been talking about a parachute anecdote used in our publication, *Hell's Best Kept Secret,* to illustrate the *motive* for putting on the Lord Jesus Christ. This is what the Christian said, "Is this a good sign when they react like this—I mean, he seemed to be enjoying the story rather nicely, until I presented the Law."

It seems obvious that the man came under conviction *because* he suddenly understood what was being said. The same thing happened to Felix the Governor, as Paul reasoned with him about righteousness, temperance, and judgment. History tells us that Felix was living in adultery, and that's why he "trembled," but instead of storming off, he had Paul removed.

Stephen's listeners were congenial until he told them that they had broken the Law (Acts 9:53). Ignorance is a cozy cloak for the guilty, that's what Jesus was saying when He said that if He hadn't spoken to them they wouldn't have had sin—"but now they have no cloak for their sin."

The words of the Lord during this time were words of warning of the coming hatred, and words of consolation that the Holy Spirit would come and help them be true and faithful witnesses to what they had seen and heard.

As times get more difficult for Christians, we mustn't let anything deter us from our mandate to be faithful witnesses. I find I need to pray for God's help every step of the way, because I am easily diverted. Late in 1993, I left the airline counter at Long Beach airport feeling disappointed that my two free upgrade certificates didn't qualify me for first class. I needed three, and I had only two, so I consoled myself with the thought that perhaps God wanted me to sit next to, and speak to someone in the economy section.

As I sat in the plane, I noticed that only two people were in an entire row, myself and a man across the aisle from me. Without warning, he sneezed seven times then went to sleep. I was fully aware that a sneeze exits at 120 m.p.h. and spreads 16 feet of germs, so I quickly moved across to the empty seat by the window, as far away as I could possibly get. As far as I was concerned, someone else could talk to Snow White's friend.

I was a little surprised at how my interest in his eternal well-being could be blown away by a mere seven sneezes. Suddenly, I wasn't too Happy that I had so little concern for Sneezie. The incident reminded me of the time when a non-Christian woman opened a door and said, "Do you believe God can protect you from diseases?" I nodded. So she barged in saying, "Good, because I have suspected infectious hepatitis." I lived through that incident, and after a little thought, I was sure I would live through this one. I knew that recent discoveries have revealed that viruses are contracted, not through the air, but through the human touch, so I felt safe.

As I sat in my seat, I began thinking of the biblical precedent of seven sneezes, and felt convicted that perhaps this was a divine encounter, so I moved back so that I could speak with him.

As I looked at this spreader of 112 feet of germs sit with his eyes closed and mouth open, I began thinking that he had a likeable face despite his nose. When he woke up, I leaned across the aisle and asked him where he was from.

When he told me, I asked him what he did for a job. He replied that he was an accountant, and asked what I did. I told him I was an author, and gave him a complimentary copy of my book, *My Friends Are Dying*. When he gave me one of his business cards, I gave him two IQ card tracts in exchange, and from there spent some time sharing the way of salvation with him. He was very open and seemed thankful that I had taken the time to speak with him. I moved back to my window seat.

I sneezed once, just as the plane landed at a stop-over. Still, I felt safe because I knew that viruses come through the human touch, not through the air . . . *and I hadn't touched him.* As the man left his seat, he leaned right over to me and shook my hand (with his).

When the flight continued, I listened to a baby scream its lungs out in the first class section, and thanked God for His clean and guiding hand.

On the way home, I sat next to a dear old lady in her eighties, who also blew me away, but this was with her breath, which reminded me of our old chicken coop from the second it hit me. She was sitting in the window seat and even the breath-taking view didn't help. She was partly deaf, which meant that when I spoke with her I was able to aim towards her ear, and wasn't forced to face the forefront of the fowl fragrance front on. This time it wasn't a nose that discouraged my witness, but a mouth.

When I gave her one of my books, it was a public presentation because she bellowed, "That's nice . . . I'm tickled to death," and kept patting the book on its cover. She said she and her daughters would read it, then she would put it away for a "keepsake." She had three daughters and kept saying things in threes. When she saw a picture of my kids she said, "Cute, cute, cute." When we arrived she said, "Well, well, well," and that talking together had been "Fun, fun, fun." Strange, strange, strange . . .

Chapter Sixteen
The Coming Persecution

Jesus spoke of the coming persecution the disciples would suffer. The purpose in this was so that they would not stumble when trials came. The devil knows that ignorance is a dark shadow which causes many to fall into a pit of despair. He also knows that knowledge is a bright lit path for the feet of the righteous, which shines more and more as we approach the "perfect day."

If the disciples knew that people would kill them thinking they were doing God a service, then when persecution came, His words would be a strong consolation for them.

Those who come under the iron fist of oppression know that those who wield the fist, do so because they don't know

God or the Savior.

Understandably, the disciples became depressed at such seeming pessimism. They had just experienced the triumph of Jerusalem's praise, and suddenly Jesus speaks of betrayal, persecution, death and the fact that He was about to leave them.

He previously told His disciples that it was necessary for Him to be glorified before the Holy Spirit was given (John 7:39). Again He tells them the same thing—that it was expedient for Him to leave, so that the Holy Spirit would come to them. The word "expedient" means that it was to their advantage that He go away. As much as His physical presence was advantageous to them, there was great benefit in His departure. The reason for this is clear when we look closely at the Tabernacle of the Old Testament, particularly the ministry of the high priest, because we see from scripture that the tabernacle was a "shadow" of the Heavenly Tabernacle (Hebrews 8:5).

When the high priest brought his offering for sin before the Lord to make atonement for himself and for his house, he was to take "coals of fire from the altar before the Lord, with his hands full of sweet incense beaten fine, and bring it inside the veil" (Leviticus 16:11-12).

The moment the Lamb of God was slain, the veil ripped in two, from the top to the bottom, signifying that atonement had been made for the Adamic race (Matthew 27:51). The way had been made for Jesus Christ, the High Priest of our faith (Hebrews 9:11), to enter the Holy of Holies and make intercession for His people (Hebrews 9:24). Like the priest of the Old Testament, He was now to take the burning coals of the Holy Spirit from the Altar of God, and baptize His disciples with "the Holy Spirit and fire," as foretold by John the Baptist (Matthew 3:11).

When the Holy Spirit was poured out on the Day of Pentecost, there appeared above their heads "cloven tongues as of fire" (Acts 2:3). A similar thing happened to the prophet in Isaiah 6:1-8. A burning coal was taken with tongs from the altar of God and used to touch Isaiah's lips and purge his sins.

That's what happened at Pentecost. The disciples not only had their sins forgiven, but their lips were touched that day and they began to speak with new-found boldness. The unspeakable blessing of life eternal being granted to sinful man happened because there was now a

High Priest, an "Advocate" seated at the right hand of the throne on High, making intercession for them (Acts 2:33, Romans 8:34).

Now their prayers could be carried "as sweet incense beaten fine" inside the veil of the presence of a Holy God. When the Holy Spirit came He would testify of Jesus, and convict the world of sin, of righteousness and of Judgment.

Conviction of Sin

There are those who think that sinners will be punished for the "sin" of failing to believe in Jesus. While it is true that those who see the light and reject it, are more guilty than those who are in ignorance, there is another aspect to this verse. According to scripture the definition of sin is not "failure to believe in Jesus," but "transgression of the Law" (1 John 3:4).

Sinners will be condemned because they don't trust the Savior, *and therefore come under the wrath of the Law for their own sins.*

If a man jumps out of a plane without a parachute, he reaps horrific consequences, *not primarily because he failed to put on the parachute,* but because he broke the law of gravity.

Those who fail to "put on the Lord Jesus Christ" will suffer the horrific consequences of sin, which may include sinful rejection of the Savior. Remember, sinners are condemned *before* they reject Jesus.

Jesus told them that when the Holy Spirit came, He would convict of righteousness "because I go to the Father and you see me no more." The Holy Spirit would be able to come because Jesus would be the Advocate in the presence of the Father. The ministry of the Holy Spirit is to convict the world of righteousness. He would show them the gap between sin and righteousness, and how that "gap" demands judgment.

When a Christian faithfully sows the seed of the Word of God, the Holy Spirit "brings the increase." He causes the seed of the truth of the Gospel to come alive in the heart of the sinner, bringing a sense of conviction and certainty of judgment to come.

The Holy Spirit convinces the world of judgment, "because the ruler of this world is judged." When Jesus died on the cross, He not only stripped the devil of his power to accuse the righteous, but He also sealed the fate of satan and his angels by purchasing redemption for the human race alone. He brought a sword of His own blood between Adam's race and his spiritual father. All who are divided from the devil by the blood of Christ, escape the judgment that will come to him and his followers (Matthew 25:41).

Probably, most of what Jesus was telling His disciples was, at that time, above their understanding, but these things were also written for *our* admonition.

The Holy Spirit would bring them back to the remembrance of the disciples at the right time.

Catastrophic

A New Jersey woman once took a large pile of washing out of her washing machine, put it down for a moment, then lifted it into her clothes drier. It was then she heard an unusual sound coming from the machine. She opened it up and pulled out "Dakota," her somewhat giddy, but drier cat, who had been taking a quick spin in the drier.

The disciple's heads must have also been spinning, after listening to Jesus speak. When He spoke of them being parted, then said "a little while and you will see Me," their confusion is understandable. They asked Him what He meant by the term, so He warned them that the world would rejoice while they wept and lamented, but their sorrow would be turned into joy.

He likened His death and resurrection to childbirth when a woman's "hour" had come. This was His hour, but like a woman, He would bear the pain because of what would be born from it. His suffering would give humanity a new birth into a new life.

Conditional Love?

As I mentioned earlier, I speak regularly to Mexicans, and I tend to use colloquialisms and cliches which aren't easy to translate. For example, the following incident may make sense in English, but imagine trying to interpret it word for word:

"One day, right *out of the blue*, I decided to take my wife to an *upper crust* Hollywood restaurant. I arrived first, and had *my eye on a particular seat*, so I sat on it and waited for my *better half*.

"I began to get worried when Sue

didn't show up, so *I pulled myself together*, then got up *to stretch my legs*.

"When she did arrive, it *took forever* for us to *catch the waiter's eye* and get service. It seemed that *every Tom, Dick and Harry* was served before us. We were in a hurry, so I ordered a hamburger and told the waiter *to step on it*. He *bent over backwards* to help us, but did we have to *pay through the nose* for the service!

"After seeing the bill, both of us felt *down in the mouth*, but we decided to *face the music* and pay it. In fact, their loud music *drove us up the wall*, so we *ate humble pie*, *hightailed* it out of there early in the evening and *hit the road*. I know *there's more than one way to skin a cat;* next time we would go elsewhere.

"Later on, we realized that if you want good service, you have to pay for it, and ended up *laughing our heads off* about the incident, realizing that *you can't have your cake and eat it too*."

When Jesus spoke to his disciples, they no longer felt as though they needed an interpreter. No longer did He speak in mystical, parabolic heavenly idioms.

He said that the Father Himself loved them because they loved the Son. Does God then not love us until we love the Savior? No, the Bible tells us that while we were yet sinners, God's love was displayed when Christ died for us. It would seem that Jesus is saying that the Father's heart *warms* to those who are obedient to the Son.

Something about this plainness of speech caused the disciples to have an increase of faith in His words; now they could trust in Him no matter what the future held for them. However, the hour would come when all of them would scatter, leaving Jesus alone with the Father.

Each of these things were said to the disciples that they might have peace. In the world they would have tribulation, but they were to be of good cheer, because He had "overcome the world." What a statement! He was telling them to take courage, because He had conquered the world. The devil had nothing on Jesus. He had no claim on Him, the world had no attraction to Him, nor was His flesh corrupted by sin. The world was beneath His feet, and "whosoever is born of God overcomes the world: and this is the victory that overcomes the world, even our faith. Who is he that overcomes the world, but he that believes that Jesus is the Son of God?" (1 John 5:4-5).

Chapter Seventeen
The Lord's Prayer

The verses in Chapter Seventeen of the Gospel of John give us insight into the prayer-life of Jesus of Nazareth. This is the true *Lord's Prayer*, as the traditional Lord's Prayer was in substance the *disciple's prayer*, as it was given to the disciples.

Jesus began by lifting His eyes up to Heaven. This is an acknowledgment that our God reigns. It reminds us that, despite our circumstances, God is in Heaven, therefore those who trust Him need not fear on earth. The opened eyes of the Savior also remind us that God is omnipresent, and to consequently rid ourselves of the erroneous notion that we are to be devout only when we close our eyes and bow in prayer.

Jesus then acknowledged that the hour of which He had so often spoke, the time for which He had been born, had finally come. He asked God to glorify Him, that He in turn might glorify God. His prayer recognized that:

1. God gave Him authority over all flesh.

2. He gave eternal life to as many as the Father had given Him.

3. Eternal life came through knowing Him and the Father.

4. He had glorified the Father and finished the work given Him.

5. Prior to His incarnation, He had majesty with the Father.

6. He had manifested God's name to those given to Him.

7. Those given to Jesus kept the Father's word.

8. Those given to Him knew that Jesus came from God.

9. Those who belonged to the Son also belonged to the Father.

10. He was glorified in His disciples.

11. God would keep them through His name.

12. None were lost except the "son of perdition."

13. His joy would be fulfilled in His disciples.

14. The world hated them because they were not of the world.

Jesus did not pray for the world directly. His prayer was that God would not take the disciples out of the world, but keep them from the evil one. He prayed for their sanctification through the truth of God's Word, and that future believers may be one as Jesus and His Father are one, so that the world then might believe.

I once spent three hours pouring my heart out to a man on a plane. As the flight was beginning to descend, he said, "O.K., so we have broken the Ten Commandments. Couldn't God have then said, `You have broken the Commandments, but I have done something to make everything right again?'" I prayed for patience and said, "That's what I have been telling you for the last three hours!"

Still, this man leaned over and said, "When I stand before God, I'm going to ask Him a few questions—across the table-like. I will say, `How come you put it in a book, and had it translated? Why didn't you just tell us what you wanted us to know.' And God will say, `There's a man who wants to know the truth.' "

His reasoning was typical of the unregenerate, whose understanding is darkened, with no fear of God or knowledge of his own moral standing before his Creator. As far as he was concerned, the issue on Judgment Day won't be his transgression against the Law of God, but a man to man question and answer time between him and God. It will be a time when God gives an overdue explanation to him as to why He did things the way He did.

This prayer of the Savior gives us some understanding into the unspeakable reverence we should have when we approach the Great White Throne, and speak to Him from whose face the heaven and earth flee away.

Chapter Eighteen
Why the Army?

When Jesus finished praying, He and His disciples made their way to the Garden of Gethsemane. Judas was familiar with the place because he often went there with Jesus and the disciples, and rightly concluded that that's where He would be. So he went there with a detachment of troops, with officers and the chief priests and the Pharisees. The Greek word used here is *speira*, meaning a military cohort of 600 men. *Why did Judas need a small army to arrest Jesus?* Did he think that the disciples would become violent? Perhaps he had seen Peter become fiery-eyed before, and thought that he would fight for Jesus. Perhaps he heard Jesus tell his disciples to love their enemies, and to turn the other cheek in the face of violence, but didn't believe that Jesus would actually practice what He preached. Maybe He would do one of His miracles and just disappear. Whatever the case, Judas wasn't taking chances.

Suddenly, this one Jesus called a "devil" was face to face with the One he called "Lord." When Jesus stepped forward and asked who they were seeking, they told Him they were seeking Jesus of Nazareth, and He responded by saying "I AM."

Almost every translation says that Jesus said to them, "I am *He*," and has the word "He" in italics, which means it wasn't in the original Greek. In Exodus 3:14, when Moses asked for God's Name, he was told to say, "**I AM** has sent me to you." The Hebrew word for AM is *Hayah*, meaning "to exist." When Jesus said to the Pharisees, "Before Abraham was, I AM," the Greek word used is *Eimi*, meaning "I exist," *and the same word* Eimi *is used in this verse*. Jesus wasn't merely identifying Himself as Jesus of Nazareth, He was affirming His deity, that He was the **I AM**, the self-existent God of Abraham, Isaac and Jacob.

The power of the name of God on the lips of Jesus caused Judas, the officers, the chief priests, at least one servant, and the whole detachment of troops to draw back and fall on the ground.

One would think that after experiencing such a supernatural thing, they would all fall on their faces and worship Him.

Suddenly, a fiery-eyed Peter drew a sword and cut off the right ear of the high priest's servant. It was obvious that this likeable and faithful fisherman hadn't understood all that Jesus had foretold him of this hour. He had been given a cup by His Father—a cup He was going to drink, no matter how bitter the taste.

Peter's Denial

When the Lamb of God was bound and taken to be examined by the High Priest, Peter and John followed at a distance.

A young servant girl who kept the door asked Peter if he was one of the disciples, to which Peter replied, "I am not." She was the keeper of the door, and in a sense, Peter was also a keeper of the door. Here before him was a door of opportunity to be a true and faithful witness of Jesus, but as this young girl tried to push open the door, he slammed it in her face.

He had cut off one servant's ear with

his sword, now he was cutting off another servant's ear by his silence. Perhaps the servant girl was seeking the salvation of God. Perhaps she had heard about this Jesus and had prayed to the God of her fathers that she may someday meet, someone who knew this Man from Nazareth, who healed the sick and raised the dead.

Peter was the one who had said, "You alone have the words of everlasting life." He was the one who had seen Jesus transfigured on the Mount, and heard the voice of Almighty God affirm that Jesus was the Son of God. Peter was one who had heard Jesus tell him he would catch men, and this was his opportunity to confess the Savior. Yet, he denied even knowing Him, and in doing so, he bore false witness.

Who of us who know the Lord, cannot identify with Peter? We have felt the paralyzing power of the fear of man grip our hearts and fasten our lips. Peter stood by the fire and warmed his cold body, but what he really needed was a fiery coal from the altar of God to touch his frozen lips.

From where Peter stood, perhaps he could hear the words spoken to Jesus by the High Priest. Maybe he heard Jesus answer him, and saw one of the officers slap Him across the face with the palm of his hand for what he decided was contempt.

Others begin to push the door of opportunity for Peter, and again he slams it shut. Three denials, and suddenly the cock crowed and woke Peter from his fear-filled nightmare.

In John 18:13, we see that Jesus was taken to Annas first, for he was the father-in-law of Caiaphas "who was High Priest that year." Yet, we find in verse 19 of the same chapter, that "the High Priest then asked Jesus of His disciples and of His doctrine."

After that, verse 24 tells us that Annas then sent Jesus bound to Caiaphas the High Priest. *Has scripture made a mistake?* Israel had only one High Priest, and yet it seems here that there were two!

This was the Day of Preparation, when the lamb was prepared for sacrifice. The High Priest had special preparation for this service. He had left his own home and made the temple his residence seven days before the preparation.

During this week he practiced his various priestly duties, such as the sprinkling of blood, the lighting of candles, the burning of incense, etc., and during this time a substitute High Priest was provided in the case that he died before the day of preparation, or that he became Levitically unclean.

Annas, his father-in-law, was his substitute.

The Beginning of Pilate's Nightmare

The "trial" of Jesus was then pitched into Pilate's court. Of course, the Pharisees didn't go into the Roman Praetorium because this would defile them, so that they couldn't eat of the passover lamb. They strained a minuscule gnat and swallowed a mammoth dinosaur. While in the process of breaking the Law by murdering the Son of God, they strove to keep the Law by separating themselves from the Gentiles. They were like twisted King Herod, who murdered John the Baptist, so that he might keep his word to his guests.

Here began a nightmare for Pontius Pilate the Governor. He commenced with a simple question as to the charge they had against Jesus. Their reply was, "If He were not a criminal, we would not have delivered Him up to you." They didn't answer directly because they couldn't.

Pilate took a closer look at the Lamb. When he asked Him if He was the King of the Jews, Jesus asked him if he heard it from someone, or if he himself was interested.

When Jesus spoke of His Kingdom not being a part of this world, and when He mentioned the word truth, Pilate's answer is sad rhetoric. Sad, because if he had pressed his "What is truth?", he would have discovered that the very embodiment of truth stood before him in human form.

One of the best advertisements for junk food are the pale faces of those who serve in health food stores. Their lack of the joy of living doesn't exactly make me want to eat food that tastes like sawdust. Their testimony sends me in the opposite direction.

One of the best advertisements for the truth of the Gospel, are the lifestyles and deathstyles of those who *deny* that truth. Their testimony should send us in the opposite direction. One man in this category, who changed the course of history because of his beliefs once said,

"It is a great satisfaction for me to find myself totally foreign to the world of Christianity. I shall never believe that what is founded on lies can endure forever. I believe in truth."

Those were the words of Adolf Hitler.

The Lamb for the Goats

Pilate then went back to the Jews and said, "I find no fault in Him at all." Let Pilate and every human court examine Jesus of Nazareth with the finest of a fine-toothed comb, and see if there is a speck of sin on the spotless Son, and they will be forced to say, "I find no fault in Him!"

Pilate then tried to appease the anger of the crowd by showing them the foolishness of their desire to put Jesus to death. He made them an offer they couldn't refuse. He would let them choose between a murderous robber, Barabbas, and this obviously innocent Man.

In the ceremonial ritual of the tabernacle, a goat was led away into the wilderness and set free, symbolizing the carrying away of Israel's sins which God had forgiven (Leviticus 16:10). Jesus used the goat as being symbolic of the wicked (Matthew 25:32), and perhaps the freeing of Barabbas is to remind us that the innocent Lamb of God was dying for the sins of the whole world, represented by this murderer and robber. The innocent suffered, while the guilty were set free. The name Barabbas means "son of the father." Barabbas was a son of the devil, and Jesus was the Son of God.

Chapter Nineteen
Misguided Pilate

It was plain that the direction this Pilate was taking was not a good one, and he knew it. He could see that it was going to land him on ground he preferred not to touch. He tried vainly to alter his course by having Jesus scourged, in the hope that it would appease the Jews. After the whipping, the twisted soldiers twisted a crown of thorns and put it on His head. This was perhaps symbolic of the Messiah taking upon Himself the curse placed upon creation when Adam fell (Genesis 3:18).

Freeways in California have their lanes divided by something called "Bott's dots." These are "bumps" originally invented by a Mr. Bott who worked the state's transit department. Between every few "dots" are small square objects which are embedded into the freeway. These are the "cat's eyes" which glow at night to help motorists keep within the lanes. However, few people know that the opposite sides of the cat's eyes are made of luminous red reflectors. If someone enters an off-ramp thinking it is actually an on-ramp, each cat's eye becomes a red warning light to tell him he is heading in the wrong direction.

Pontius Pilate had a red warning light every time he turned a corner. Good sense, conscience and even his wife, who cautioned him that what he was doing was unjust (Matthew 27:19), were all signs warning him that he was heading in the wrong direction.

After they placed a purple robe on Jesus, mocked Him as a king, struck Him with their hands, ripped His beard from His face and spat upon Him (fulfilling Isaiah 50:6), Pilate came out again to the crowd and said,

> "Behold I am bringing Him out to you, that you may know I find no fault in Him."

It was the passover. The Lamb of God was being prepared for sacrifice, and was declared to be without blemish.

Jesus had been cruelly scourged,

Pilate's soldiers had further beaten Him, and on top of that, he told the Jews that Jesus was innocent. Surely the case would be closed, but as soon as their eyes set upon Jesus, they screamed for His blood. Again Pilate said that he found no fault in Him, and told them to take Him and crucify Him themselves. When the Pharisees said that it was the Law of God that demanded His death, he became even more afraid. This public prosecution was progressing into a personal and pestilent predicament for poor Pontius Pilate.

When the Governor went back into the praetorium and questioned Jesus, He "opened not His mouth" (Isaiah 53:7). When Pilate reminded Him that he had the power to crucify Him or to release Him, Jesus reminded him that God was on the throne, and every breath he took came only by His permission. He even seemed to sympathize with Pilate in his predicament, saying that he who delivered Him to Pilate had the greater sin. From then on, the Governor sought to release Jesus, but the Jews put further pressure on him, saying that to side with Jesus was treasonous to Rome.

When Pilate heard that, he brought Jesus out into a place paved with mosaic stones, and sat down on his judgment seat. The mosaic stones were laid a little higher than the surrounding area, signifying how all who stand in judgment under the Mosaic Law will be set forth publicly. Pontius Pilate was a puppet of the people, swayed like a weak bowed tree by the winds of the spirit of murder. He grossly underestimated the hatred man has for God, and when he changed his "Behold the Man!" to "Behold your King!" they further howled like ravaging animals for His blood. The pressure was so intense, when they proclaimed allegiance to Caesar rather than to God to strengthen their own case for His crucifixion, Pilate granted them their wish.

The Lamb is Sacrificed

How could this nightmare be happening! Never had there been such goodness in human form; never such kindness, decency and virtue in one Man.

Yet, Jesus of Nazareth was being led away as a criminal to be nailed to a cross. He was to be held high as a lawbreaker, a criminal, warning the world as to what would happen to those who did as this Man did.

Two others were crucified with Him, one on either side, and Jesus in the center.

Pilate, as a gesture of distaste for what the Jews had forced his trembling hand to do, had placed a sign on the cross, saying,

JESUS OF NAZARETH,

KING OF THE JEWS.

At the foot of the cross, the soldiers divided His garments and gambled for His tunic, fulfilling scripture (Psalm 22:18). It was at the foot of the cross that the robe of Christ was divided into four pieces. It would also be at the foot of the cross that sinners from the four corners of the earth would humbly bow, and be robed with garment of His righteousness.

Even while Jesus hung in agony on the cross, He showed love and concern for the welfare of His mother, committing her into the hands of John.

As one last gesture of human enmity, when Jesus cried "I thirst!", He was given vinegar to drink.

Psalm 22:16 speaks of the Messiah's hands and feet being pierced, giving a unique and horrifying insight into the suffering of the Messiah:

1. He was aware of their scorning (verses 6-7).

2. He could hear the mocking words

(verse 8).

3. He was praying (verses 9-13).

4. The strain of crucifixion dragged his bones out of joint (verse 14).

5. Loss of blood made his heart feel as though it was melting (verse 14).

6. His strength totally left Him (verse 15).

7. Thirst caused His tongue to adhere to His mouth (verse 15).

8. He could see them gambling for His clothes (verse 18).

When He had received the vinegar, He cried, "It is finished!" Finally, the debt had been paid. The blood of the perfect Lamb of God had been shed for sinful man. The demands of the Law of God had been satisfied by the suffering of Jesus of Nazareth. He bowed His head, and gave up His spirit.

The Hands of a Carpenter

This was a special day for Israel. It was the Day of Preparation, and the distasteful events that preceded it needed to be dealt with and forgotten.

The Jews asked Pilate to break the legs of the criminals and hurry their death, so that the bodies wouldn't remain on the crosses on such a holy day.

But when they came to Jesus, they found that He was already dead, so a soldier thrust a sword into His side, just to make sure.

Then the Scriptures tell us that Joseph of Arimathaea "being a disciple of Jesus, but secretly for fear of the Jews, asked Pilate that he might take away the body of Jesus" (John 19:38).

Joseph was a captive of his own fears. He was *snared* by the fear of man. The honor of his own name in the sight of his contemporaries, was more important to him than the honor that comes from God. He preferred the praises of men, to the praises of God.

But something happened to him that day. A sense of shame gripped him as he stood with the multitude at the foot of the cross, and heard the cries of Jesus of Nazareth. Light pierced his soul, as darkness covered the land. It was as though God enshrouded Golgotha with blackness, so the world could not see the agonies of His Son, as the gavel of His fury came down upon the sacrifice. In the blackness, the eyes of Joseph of Arimathaea saw "Jesus Christ evidently set forth and crucified."

It wasn't only the seven sayings of the Savior that swayed his soul. There was the unforgettable statement that came from the lips of the Roman centurion. The man heard Jesus cry out with a loud voice, breath his last, and with widened eyes this death-hardened Gentile soldier "feared greatly" and uttered, *"Truly this Man was the Son of God!"*

Joseph was a witness of a drama he didn't want to see. As each incident unfolded, it became embedded upon his unwilling mind. He watched in horror as stone-hearted Romans did their grisly task, and he heard the unforgettable echoes of the hammer striking the nails as they pierced holy flesh, and sunk deep into the wood of the cross. His mind reeled at the callousness of the soldiers as they gambled for the seamless robe, and he witnessed the blasphemy and the cruel mockings of the chief priests and the scribes.

He also had the indelible memory of seeing the face of the mother of Jesus, as a sword pierced her soul. This was a day he would not, *could not* easily forget.

The blackness, the earthquake, the sobering words from the cross and from the centurion, put a healthy fear of God in the heart of Joseph, and stirred him to make a decision to either live for God, or live for man. He boldly went to Pilate and pleaded for the body of Jesus. Each of the four Gospels relates this incident.

Ugly Birds

Another was there on that dreadful day. It was he who "first came to Jesus by night"—Nicodemus, the leader of the Jews. Three times the Gospel of John tells us that Nicodemus came by night, inferring that perhaps he too, had a problem with the fear of man. This time, he didn't come in the dark. He too had been given light, and he no longer cared what the Pharisees thought. They stood afar off, in their proud self-righteousness, like ugly vultures after they had picked a carcass to the bone.

Nicodemus had heard gracious words that came from the mouth of this Man from Nazareth on the first night he visited Him. He knew that He came from God. Years earlier, the words of the Savior were life to him as they found residence within his heart. They seemed to echo with stark reality, as he looked up at the cross:

"As Moses lifted up the serpent in the wilderness, even so must the Son of Man be lifted up, that whoever believes in Him should not perish but have everlasting life."

As he gazed upon the gruesome sight, how could he be ashamed of Jesus of Nazareth, *knowing that this was the sacrificial Lamb of God!* In the light of the cross, he became dead to the world, and the world to him.

It was Joseph of Arimathaea who had the honor of taking the body of Jesus down from the cross (Luke 23:53). But think for a moment what it would be like to have to pull the cold and lifeless hands of the Son of God from the thick, barbed, Roman nails. These were the carpenter's hands, which once held nails and wood, now were being held by nails and wood. These were the hands that broke bread and fed multitudes, now being broken to feed multitudes. They once applied clay to a blind man's eyes, touched lepers, healed the sick, washed the disciple's feet, and took children in His arms. These were the hands that more than once, loosed the cold hand of death, now held firmly by its icy grip.

These were the fingers that wrote in the sand when the adulterous woman was cast at His feet, and for the love of God, fashioned a whip that purged His Father's House. These were the same fingers that took bread and dipped it in a dish, and gave it to Judas as a gesture of deep love and friendship. Here was the Bread of Life itself, being dipped in the cup of suffering, as the ultimate gesture of God's love for the evil world that Judas represented.

Joseph's shame, that he had been afraid to own the Savior, sickened him as he tore the blood-sodden feet from the six inch cold steel spike that fastened them to the cross. These were the "beautiful feet" of Him that preached the Gospel of peace, that Mary washed with her hair, that walked upon the Sea of Galilee, now crimson with a sea of blood.

As Joseph reached out his arms to get Him down from the cross, he stared for an instant at the inanimate face of the Son of God. His heart wrenched as he looked upon Him whom they had pierced. This face, which once radiated with the glory of God on the Mount of Transfiguration, which so many had looked upon with such veneration, was now blood-stained from the needle-sharp crown of thorns, deathly pale and twisted from unspeakable suffering as the sin of the world was laid upon Him.

His eyes, which once sparkled with the life of God, now stared at nothingness, as

He was brought into the dust of death. His lips, which spoke such gracious words, and calmed the fears of so many, were swollen and bruised from the beating given to him by the hardened fists of cruel soldiers.

As it was written, "He was more marred than any man."

Perhaps Nicodemus reached up to help Joseph with the body. As the cold blood of the Lamb of God covered his hands, he was reminded of the blood of the passover lamb he had seen shed so many times. The death of each spotless animal had been so quick and merciful, but this death had been unspeakably cruel, vicious, inhuman, and brutal. It seemed that all the hatred that sin-loving humanity had for the Light, formed itself into a dark and evil spear, and was thrust with cruel delight into the perfect Lamb of God.

As he carefully pried the crown from His head, looked at the gaping hole in His side, the deep mass of abrasions upon His back, and the mutilated wounds in His hands and feet, a sense of outrage engrossed him, that this could happen to such a Man as this. But the words of the Prophet Isaiah rang within his heart:

"He was wounded for *our* transgressions, he was bruised for *our* iniquities . . . the Lord has laid upon Him the iniquity of us all . . . as a lamb to the slaughter . . . for the transgression of My people He was stricken . . . yet it pleased the Lord to bruise Him . . . by His knowledge shall My righteous servant justify many."

Jesus of Nazareth was stripped of His robe, that we might be robed in pure righteousness. He suffered a deathly thirst, that our thirst for life might be quenched. He agonized under the curse of the Law, that we might relish the blessing of the Gospel. He took upon Himself the hatred of the world, so that we could experience the love of God. Hell was let loose upon Him, so that Heaven could be let loose upon us. Jesus of Nazareth tasted the bitterness of death, so that we might taste the sweetness of life everlasting. The Son of God willingly passed over His life, that death might freely pass over the sons and daughters of Adam.

May Calvary's cross be as real to us as it was to those who stood on its bloody soil on that terrible day. May we also gaze upon the face of the crucified Son of God, and may shame grip our hearts if ever the fear of man comes near our souls. May we identify with the Apostle Paul, who could have gloried in his dramatic and miraculous experience on the Road to Damascus. Instead he whispered in awe of God's great love:

> "God forbid that I should glory, save in the cross of our Lord Jesus Christ, by whom the world is crucified unto me, and I unto the world."

The Warning

After five years of experimentation, and at an estimated cost of $2,000,000,000, the United States developed the first atomic bomb, which was successfully tested in New Mexico on July 16, 1945. The Japanese were informed of the bomb and told to surrender. Their reaction was to say that the ultimatum was unworthy of their notice.

At 9:15 a.m. on Monday August 6, 1945, an atomic bomb was dropped on the Japanese city of Hiroshima, instantly killing 78,000 people, wounding 100,000 and destroying 4.1 square miles, 60% of the city.

Still the Japanese refused to surrender. So, three days later, another bomb was dropped on the city of Nagasaki, bringing five years of horror, World War Two, to a final end.

The cross of Jesus Christ is a fearful warning to humanity. Throughout history, the prophets, at the spilling of their own blood, have forewarned that God will punish sin, yet many in Israel scoffed at the thought of Judgment Day—the warning was unworthy of their notice. The first bomb was dropped 2,000 years ago when the Savior died. So serious is our Creator about iniquity, He poured His fury upon the Messiah, not only to demonstrate His love for humanity, but also to illustrate His righteousness. Today we have both the warning of the prophets and the demonstration of the cross. Still, to our shame, most consider the ultimatum unworthy of their notice.

Chapter Twenty
Body Snatchers!

I can't imagine any of those who loved Jesus sleeping too well that night. The events of the day had been an unspeakably horrific nightmare for the godly, but for those who loved evil, they had been a dream come true. No doubt the Jews who wanted Him crucified slept well. Rest assured, they had their heart's desire.

Mary Magdalene decided she would go to the tomb early in the morning while it was still dark. It unquestionably was dark. Life couldn't have cast a darker more solemn shadow. A few days earlier, life which seemed so sweet, had suddenly turned bitter to the uttermost. *What more could go wrong?*

At least she had the consolation of

being able to go to the tomb of her beloved Lord and shed her grief there.

Suddenly, even that was taken from her by body snatchers. She ran and told Peter and John that someone had taken the body.

They ran to the tomb, and stooping down saw an incredible sight. The strips of linen, which Nicodemus and Joseph of Arimathaea had wrapped around the body were lying there, but the napkin which had been around His head was lying separate, and folded together in a place by itself.

This is not the way of body snatchers! They don't meticulously take strips of linen off a body, then carefully unwind the napkin from around the head, fold it, and place it by itself! Perhaps over the years, they had witnessed the habits of Jesus. After every meal, He would fold His napkin neatly, and then place it to one side. Perhaps they had seen him fold the towels one after another, after He washed His disciple's feet.

Whatever the case, the arrangement of the linen cloths contributed in some way to them believing that Jesus had risen from the dead, because they didn't know at that point of time that the Scriptures said He would rise from the dead.

There is another thought. The linen was in a shambles, but the napkin from the head was folded neatly. The Body of Christ is at present enshrouded in fine linen (Revelation 19:8), and in the sight of the world, the Church is in disarray. However, Christ the Head (Colossians 1:18) is totally in order, enthroned in Heaven.

The two disciples went home, but Mary wasn't comforted. She stood outside the tomb weeping. Through her tears, she also stooped down and looked into the tomb, but instead of seeing what the disciples saw, she saw two angels in white, one sitting at the head and the other at the feet of where Jesus had laid. When they inquired as to the reason for her sorrow, she said it was because the body of her Lord had been removed from the tomb.

When she had said this, she turned around and saw Jesus, but she didn't know it was Him. Perhaps tears clouded her eyes, or more than likely, the glorified Savior looked and sounded different after the resurrection. In Luke's Gospel, two disciples didn't know that it was Jesus who spoke to and walked with them on the road to Emmaus (Luke 24:13).

It was when Jesus said Mary's name

that she turned around and said *"Rabboni!"* As her name was spoken, suddenly her darkness turned to light, and her agony to unspeakable joy. Her nightmare became a dream. In that one spoken word, death lost its sting and Heaven swung open wide its glorious and golden gates, because the resurrection put Almighty God's seal of truth upon the words of Jesus of Nazareth.

The resurrection of Jesus Christ was the beginning of the end for the vile business of undertaking.

Have you heard Jesus say *your* name? Or are you merely believing something others have told you? Do you *know* the glorified Savior? Has He made His residence, through the life of His Spirit, within you? If you are not sure of your eternal salvation, let me ask you a question. Imagine if I said to you that I was working for the UCLA Medical Institute, and that our scientists, due to recent changes in the law, can now pay big money for human corneas. Here's my question: *Would you sell me one of your eyes for a million dollars?* Not only will your eye give sight to a blind person, but you will walk away with one million dollars in cool, tax-free cash. What's more, the operation is totally painless, takes less than one hour, and the new eye will look as good as the authentic one. You will look the same; but you won't *look* the same . . . one eye will be blind.

Perhaps you would sell just one eye for a million dollars. *How about selling both for fifteen million?* Think for a moment what you would do with all that money—you could see the world. Not quite. You could sit at home in the blackness of total blindness and count it. I'm sure no one in their right mind, would consider selling his or her eyesight for *fifty* million dollars!

Perhaps you have never given it any deep thought, but your eyes are utterly priceless, and yet they are merely the windows of the soul—the "life" that peers through the shutters of your eyes. If your eyes are without price, *what must your life be worth?* In fact, Jesus said that your life is so valuable, you are to actually *despise* your eyes in comparison to the worth of your soul. He said that if your right eye causes you to sin, you are to pluck it out and cast it from you, for it would be better to go to Heaven without an eye than to go to Hell blind, where the "worm never dies and the fire is never quenched." He said that the combined riches of this entire world are not worth losing your soul for: "What shall it profit a man if he gains the whole world and loses his soul?"

Tell me, what are you selling your soul for? Is it your love for sin? Does your eye feed your sinful heart on sexually explicit movies? It's your love for them that is stopping you getting right with God, and you don't want to let that pleasure go. Then it would be better for you to be utterly blind, and get right with God, than go to Hell for your love of lust. Is the hindrance your God-insulting faithlessness? Do you find it hard to believe God's promises? Then you are deeming Him not worthy of your trust. Try that one with of your friends, and see how long the friendship lasts. If you don't believe the testimony of Jesus Christ, then you are spitting in the face of the Savior with the soldiers who mocked Him, because you think He was a liar and a deceiver. Perhaps you think you are a good person, and that you don't need God's mercy? Then you are a blind, self-righteous Pharisee, and you choose to stand afar off with those vultures who crucified the Son of God. For you, He shed His precious blood in vain. His sacrifice wasn't worthy of you, so you will, therefore, have to have your own Day in Court, when every secret sin will be uncovered and show you for what you really are.

Whatever it is that is hindering your salvation, *please*, let the Law of God do its painful but precious work, and bring you to the foot of the blood-stained cross.

Let's go through the Commandments together and pray that God gives you light. With a tender conscience, answer the following: Have you ever told a lie? This includes any fibs, white lies, half-truths or exaggerations told in the past. Remember, time doesn't forgive sin! God sees the sins of your youth as though it was yesterday. If you have told even one lie, then you are a liar (be brutally honest with yourself, because God will be on the Day of Judgment). Have you ever stolen something? The value of the item is totally irrelevant. If you have stolen one thing, then you are a thief.

Have you committed murder, or have you *desired to* by harboring hatred in your heart? Jesus said if you look at someone and lust for them, then you have committed adultery in your heart (Matthew 5:27-28). Have you ever done that? Then you are an adulterer at heart. Have you had sex out of marriage, or committed adultery, or desired to? Then you have committed sexual sin and cannot enter Heaven (1 Corinthians 6:9). Have you kept the Sabbath holy, always honored your parents, have you put God first in your affections, loving Him with all your heart, mind, soul and strength? Have you always loved your neighbor as much as you have loved yourself? Most of us have trouble loving our "loved" ones, let alone loving our neighbors. Have you ever used God's name in vain, either employing it as a curse word, or failing to give it due honor? Have you made a god to suit yourself and therefore been guilty of "idolatry"—making a god in your own image, believing in your version of what you think God is like? Have you ever desired anything that belonged to someone else? If you have broken even one of these Ten Commandments, then you have sinned against God. On Judgment Day every sin you have ever committed will come out as evidence of your guilt. You will be damned forever, and lose your soul. Without God's mercy, you will go to Hell. The Scriptures warn that unless you repent, you will perish.

Through the pages of this book, you have seen the love of God in Christ poured out for you on the cross. He took the punishment which was due to you and me upon His own body and soul, so that we might be proclaimed "not guilty" on the Day we stand before the Judge of the universe. Jesus of Nazareth satisfied the demands of Eternal Justice, and at the same time He demonstrated how much God loves us. Don't wait another minute, repent and put your faith in Jesus, and God will forgive your sins and grant you the gift of everlasting life. You ask *How do I do that?* Tell God you are sorry for your sins, then go and sin no more. Think of what it cost God for you to be forgiven. Think of the suffering of the Savior. That was the price of our redemption. If you can't find the right words, open a Bible at Psalm 51, and make that your prayer to God. Then place yourself entirely in the hands of the Savior, read the Bible daily, obey it implicitly, and you will "make your calling and election sure."

Sadness to Gladness

Jesus discouraged Mary from clinging to Him. She was no longer to trust in Him in His physical person, but through the power of His Spirit. However, the Spirit would only be given if He ascended to the place of intercession for the saints as the High Priest.

Once that had taken place, God was not only His and her God, but His, and now her *Father*. Redemption would be complete for the sons and daughters of Adam. No longer would those who trusted in the atoning death of the Savior be children of the devil—God would become their Father, because they would be born into His family.

Meanwhile, as the disciples were behind locked doors for fear of the Jews, *Jesus suddenly appeared in their midst*, showing them His hands and His pierced side. Here in the Scriptures, we have what must be the understatement of the century:

"Then were the disciples glad when they saw the Lord."

All Is Well

A woman once gasped in horror at the sight before her. Her dog was wagging his tail as though nothing was wrong. In its mouth was a dirt-stained and lifeless rabbit. She recognized the dead animal as the beloved pet of her neigh-bor's young child. Her dog had obviously broken into its cage, chased the poor rabbit into the dirt, and killed the wretched creature.

Her neighbors were on a three day vacation, so she took the muddied rabbit and washed its lifeless body, then brushed its fur and put it back in its cage, so at least the family wouldn't see their dead pet in the state in which she had seen it. She felt terrible that her dog had killed it so viciously, so this was the least she could do.

When the neighbors returned home, they came and knocked on her door. She nervously opened it to see mystified neighbors. Three days earlier, they had found the rabbit dead in the cage, buried it, and now it was back, clean and fresh as a daisy! No doubt the woman was relieved.

There must have also been a great relief in the hearts of the disciples to hear Jesus say, "Fear not." His calm and loving voice banished their fears that they too, had betrayed Him by forsaking Him in the Garden of Gethsemane.

Then Jesus gave them His peace, commissioned them, breathed on them the Holy Spirit and gave them authority to proclaim forgiveness of sins. This does not mean they had the power to give absolution of sins—"who can forgive sins but God?" But as ministers of the Gospel, the Christian can boldly proclaim that those who are born of the Spirit of God have remission of sins. This is what Peter fearlessly announced on the Day of Pentecost:

"Repent and be baptized everyone of

you in the name of Jesus Christ for the remission of sins; and you shall receive the gift of the Holy Spirit" (Acts 2:38).

Why did Jesus breathe on His disciples and say, "Receive the Holy Spirit" *when He had already told them that the Holy Spirit could only come after His ascension* (John 16:7)? Perhaps it was at that moment that the Body of Christ on earth was conceived within the womb.

Perhaps it was then that He *planted* the seed of the life of the Church, but after the gestation period, on the Day of Pentecost, the Body of Christ was then *birthed* on earth.

The first seed of Adam's race began with the breath of God (Genesis 2:7), and now the "second Adam" begins with the breath of God in Christ. The first man had been formed from the dust of the ground, but when the Lord God breathed into his nostrils the breath of life, he became a "living soul." The first creation was made a living soul, but the Body of Christ was made "a quickening spirit" (1 Corinthians 15:45).

Jesus picked up fallen dust from the ground of Israel, shaped them for three years, and now He breathed life into them, as He did in Genesis with the dust

He had formed into Adam's body. It was but a gentle breath at conception, which became a rushing mighty wind on the Day of Pentecost (Acts 2:2), and caused the living Body of Christ to stand on its feet on earth.

Thomas' Timing

Thomas wasn't there when Jesus appeared to the disciples, and therefore doubted that He had risen from the dead. He wanted the undeniable evidence of putting his finger into the print of the nails, and putting his hand into the side of the Savior, before he would believe.

There was nothing wrong with wanting to see the Lord's wounds. Jesus Himself showed them to His disciples, but Thomas had a heart of unbelief. To him, the disciples were lying when they told Him they had seen Jesus.

There can be a lot of blood when a baby is born. That's probably the reason so many husbands faint at the birth. In fact, the nurse that delivered our second child ended up with blood all over her face. The doctor was late, so she did the delivery, and cut the umbilical cord in the wrong place and was sprayed with blood. She screamed, and everyone in the delivery room burst into laughter. A child had been born, and if everyone in the room had been covered in blood, it wouldn't have dampened the joy.

Can you imagine how different the atmosphere would have been if the child had been still-born? The nurse would have solemnly picked the tiny corpse in her hands, wrapped it in a towel, and walked over to the basin to wash the blood off her hands.

This blood now spoke of death rather than life, of terrible grief rather than joy.

Many times in the past I have had my joy turned to mourning. I had the delight of leading someone to the Savior, but time revealed that I had a "still-born" on my hands. I had rejoiced that someone had come to new life in Christ, but there was in truth no life of God in them. I had their blood on my hands, and the feeling wasn't a good one. I had failed to leave them in the womb of conviction, so that they would not be born of the will of man, nor of the will of the flesh, but of God.

After His resurrection, Jesus appeared to Thomas on the eighth day. Why the eighth? Babies are circumcised on the eighth day, and the reason for this is because this is the time that the coagulating factor in the blood called "prothrombin" is at its highest. Science has recently discovered that that is when the human body's immune system is at its highest. The eighth day was the God-given timing for circumcision, and there is a God-given timing for every person who is "circumcised with the circumcision not made with hands." What Thomas saw, cut away the flesh of an unbelieving heart. Thomas became a Jew inwardly. His circumcision became "that of the heart, in the Spirit, and not of the letter." He bowed his heart to Jesus of Nazareth as his Lord and his God. He needed a miracle, and God was gracious and gave it to him.

Each of us are dealt with differently; some get incredible spiritual manifestations at conversion. Others quietly trust the promises of God, and God reveals Himself to them through faith rather than feelings of great joy. What matters is not *how* each of us came to Christ, but that we became new creatures in Christ, because that is the *real* miracle, that is what proves the reality of salvation. This is what Paul was saying when he said, "For in Christ Jesus neither circumcision nor uncircumcision avails anything, but a new creature" (Galatians 6:15).

As with Thomas, each of us are also dealt with in God's timing and in God's way. Those who don't understand this will run around getting decisions for Jesus who are in truth "still-born" stony ground hearers, leaving the local pastor, whom they are trying to help, with liabilities rather than assets.

Thomas saw and believed, but Jesus proclaimed God's special blessing upon those who trust in Him and yet do not see.

Jesus did many other signs for His disciples, signs we know nothing about, but the reason we have a record of what He did do, is so that you and I might acquire salvation through faith in Jesus Christ, the Son of the Living God.

Chapter Twenty-one
Fish For Breakfast

After the Thomas affair, Jesus revealed Himself to the disciples again, this time while seven of them were fishing at the Sea of Tiberias, which is another name for the Sea of Galilee. Believe it or not, Thomas was with them this time, and not one of the disciples caught a thing that night. When morning came, Jesus stood on the shore and asked if they had any food. When they told Him they hadn't caught a thing, He said where to find the fish, and when they tried to pull the net in, they could not because it was so full.

This wasn't the first time something like this had happened. Three years earlier, Jesus was with Peter, James and John by the Lake of Gennesaret. He told Peter to "launch out into the deep and let down

your nets for a catch." Peter told Him
that they had toiled all night and caught
nothing, but he said, "nevertheless at
Your word I will let down the net." When
they did what Jesus said, they caught so
many fish that their net began to break.
They called to their partners who came
to help, but when they filled their boats,
they began to sink.

When Peter saw what happened, he
was filled with contrition, fell at Jesus'
knees and said, "Depart from me, for I
am a sinful man, O Lord!" Jesus then
said to him, "Do not be afraid. From now
on you will catch men." When they had
brought their boats to land, they forsook
all and followed Him (Luke 5:1-11).

It was Peter's idea to go fishing, and
the disciples followed him. Soon, Peter
would be the one to take a leadership
role on the Day of Pentecost. He would
work again with Jesus, but this time as a
fisher of men, and he would see a great
multitude brought into the Gospel net.
Three thousand souls would come into
the Kingdom because they would listen
to the instructions of Jesus, and wait for
the Power from on High.

The first time Peter experienced a
great catch of fish, the nets began to
break and the boats began to sink, but
after three years with Jesus, when it hap-

pened again, both the nets and the boats held,

Three thousand souls came into the Kingdom at Pentecost, because Peter had gained knowledge from Jesus on how to be a fisher of men. At Pentecost, he recognized that those who stood before him were "devout Jews from every nation under Heaven." These were godly Jews who, like Nicodemus, were thoroughly versed in the Law of their God. They knew what sin was because the Law instructed them, for sin is transgression of the Law (1 John 3:4). Had they not been godly, he no doubt would have followed in the steps of the Master and taken the time to instruct out of the Law, as Jesus did with the arrogant lawyer and with the rich young ruler (Luke 1:24, 18:18). Those who gain such valuable experience from scripture will find that they too will be true fishers of men, and they too will know the joy of pulling in the net and not losing the catch (for further teaching on this subject see our publication, *Hell's Best Kept Secret*).

When they pulled the net to the shore, they saw that Jesus had made a fire and had bread and fish laid upon it. He was into loaves and fishes. This is because the two should never be separated. Loaves speak to us of the Word of God—"Man shall not live by bread alone, but by every Word of God," and fish reminds us of the unsaved—we are to be fishers of men. Both are warmed by the fire that the Holy Spirit gives, and the more we read God's Word, the more we see our responsibility to reach out to the lost. The Holy Spirit was given at Pentecost primarily so that the disciples would be witnesses for Jesus, fishers of men (Acts 1:8).

There is a great sea of humanity that are still unsaved, and God has given us the responsibility of reaching them. Those who do so will have "meat to eat" that others know nothing of (John 4:32), and they will have a sweet, intimate breakfast with Jesus.

Do You Love Me?

Three times Peter denied Jesus, three times Jesus had revealed Himself to him and his brethren, and now Jesus asks him a question three times. Three times He asked Peter if he loved Him. In the first two instances Jesus used the word *agapao*, for love. He asked if he loved Him in a moral sense. We owe the Lord our affection, with all of our heart, mind, soul and strength, as our Maker and the One who has blessed us with food, clothing and all the pleasures this life brings.

He used the same word the second time, but the third time Jesus used the word *phileo*, which means "to be a friend." There is a big difference between loving Jesus in a moral obligatory sense, and loving Him as friend in a close tender relationship.

Notice these three questions came after they had eaten. It is when we are full and content that we are able to see how genuine our love for Jesus is. We tend to pray a lot when we are in want, but when we are full, both in the belly and in the bank, we tend to put the Lord at a distance. It is a wise Christian who will say,

> "Give me neither poverty nor riches—feed me with the food You prescribe for me: Lest I be full and deny You, and say, `Who is the Lord?' Or lest I be poor and steal, and profane the name of my God" (Proverbs 30:8-10).

Those who love the Lord Jesus as a friend will gladly follow Him wherever He goes. If He leads them to help the poor, the suffering, the blind, or to go to the highways, the byways and the hedges, they will gladly follow. If the Good Shepherd's voice is heard saying, "This is the way, walk in it," the friend of Jesus will joyfully take up his cross daily and follow Him.

In the closing verses of this Gospel, we see Peter erring yet again, perhaps for our instruction. The question that arose, was whether or not John would escape death. Yet, we are not to be concerned about how the Lord deals with other Christians. The Apostle Paul said,

> "None of us lives to himself, and none of us dies to himself. For if we live, we live to the Lord; and if we die, we die to the Lord. Therefore, whether we live or die, we are the Lord's. For to this end Christ died and rose and lived again, that He might be Lord of both the dead and the living. But why do you judge your brother? Or why do you show contempt for your brother? For we shall all stand before the Judgment Seat of Christ" (Romans 14:7-10).

John wrote this Gospel so that we might have some insight into the life of Jesus of Nazareth. Yet, when we recall everything we are told He did—His turning the water to wine, healing the blind, walking on water, raising Lazarus—we must remember these incredible miracles are only a tiny part of the miracles that issued from this Man. Never a man did the things that this Man did; never a Man spoke the gracious words that this Man spoke. He came to abolish death and bring life and immortality to light through the Gospel. This is good news, even for the undertaker who is able to see beyond his deathly income. God promised, through the prophets

"He will swallow up death in victory; and the Lord God will wipe away tears from all faces... And it shall be said in that day, Lo, this is our God; we have waited for Him, and He will save us" (Isaiah 25:8-9).

The joy will be inexpressible on that day for those who have obeyed the Gospel. They will see the fulfillment of the pledge of our Creator, when He said, "I will ransom them from the power of the grave; I will redeem them from death."

On that day "the Lord Himself shall descend from Heaven with a shout, with the voice of the archangel, and with the trump of God: and the dead in Christ shall rise first."

I pray that you have obeyed the Gospel, truly repented of all sin, and put your trust in Jesus Christ, the Son of the Living God . . . that you too have believed, and in believing found life through His name.